Praise for

You Look So Much Better in Person

Amazon, "Best Biographies & Memoirs of the Month"
USA TODAY, "Five Books Not to Miss!"
AARP, "Inspirational New Books"

"[This book is] illustrated with great charm, and [shows] that you don't have to be the company chest-beater to be the winner." —*New York Times*

"Full of amusing stories." —AARP

"A charming memoir that will inspire readers." —*Chicago Sun Times*

"[Roker] talks straight up success…" —*Washington Informer*

"This sunny, pleasant book is perfect for Roker fans or anyone in need of a quick pick me up." —*Publisher's Weekly*

"Sharing a host of lively anecdotes, Roker reflects on what he's learned from his undeniably successful career. […] Ebullient revelations of a contented life." —*Kirkus*

"An easy recommendation." —*Booklist*

"I love aphorisms, so I loved the organization of this book by 'ALtruisms'—lessons for career and life that Al Roker has learned along the way. So many great insights."
—Gretchen Rubin, author of *The Happiness Project*

YOU LOOK
SO MUCH BETTER
IN PERSON

YOU LOOK SO MUCH BETTER IN PERSON

True Stories of Absurdity and Success

AL ROKER

hachette
BOOKS

New York

Hachette Go, an imprint of Hachette Books
Hachette Book Group
1290 Avenue of the Americas
New York, NY 10104
HachetteGo.com
Facebook.com/HachetteGo
Instagram.com/HachetteGo

First trade paperback edition: July 2021

Hachette Books is a division of Hachette Book Group, Inc. The Hachette Go and Hachette Books name and logos are trademarks of Hachette Book Group, Inc.

The publisher is not responsible for websites (or their content) that are not owned by the publisher.

Editorial production by Christine Marra, *Marra*thon Production Services. www.marrathoneditorial.org

Book design by Jane Raese
Set in 12.5-point New Baskerville

Library of Congress Control Number: 2020937929

ISBN 978-0-316-42679-4 (hardcover), ISBN 978-0-306-87457-4 (large print), ISBN 978-0-316-42678-7 (ebook), 978-0-316-42680-0 (trade paperback)

Printed in the United States of America

LSC-C

10 9 8 7 6 5 4 3 2 1

Contents

Introduction

PEOPLE OFTEN ASK ME, "Al, did you always want to work in television? Did you always want to do the weather? Was it your lifelong dream to be on *The Today Show?*" The answer to those questions is No, No, and another big No. Young Coke-bottle-glasses-wearing Al Roker of the Xavier High School AV club didn't have a clue about his life's mission. He probably would have been too busy eating snacks and drawing cartoons to give much of an answer, but I can tell you I never had a plan.

Making a five-year plan was never part of my mode of operation. In fact, I think if you have a five-year plan you should consider taking a match to it. I have been forecasting the weather for forty years and I can't necessarily predict tomorrow's weather with 100 percent accuracy— how the hell would I know what I'll be doing in five years? Plans are rigid, can easily go awry, and leave little room for fun, adventure, and exploration. I credit not having a plan with some of the best developments in my life—getting my first gig in college, living in the great Midwest where I became a solid member of a team, and eventually coming full circle back to New York City when I took a part-time job at WNBC. Not having a plan forced me to work hard, be patient, stay in the long game, be flexible, and focus on what really matters, like getting good at my craft and working with good people.

I have been working for over four decades . . . four decades! And I can tell you that I've landed in a much better place than any prematurely balding kid in a polyester suit could have conceived of.

I hope that what I've shared in this book from years of working will inspire you to take it day by day rather than fret about your future. It is my wish that after reading these pages you do take a match to that plan—light it up! And instead of fretting about your future, take it step by step. I believe that if you can look in the mirror at the end of the day and honestly say you did your best—and you do it again and again—your best life will open up for you. It might not be exactly how you expected, and it might take longer than you want, but trust me, life is about something much bigger than a plan. Sit back and see where it all takes you.

Assumptions Are NOT Your Friend

IT WAS THE HEAD of the communications department at SUNY Oswego, Dr. Lewis B. O'Donnell, who gave me the tip-off about the job. WHEN-TV5 (now WTVH) was adding a 6:00 P.M. broadcast to their Saturday and Sunday schedule and was pulling together a full news team: an anchor, sports guy, and weather forecaster. The news director at WHEN, the CBS affiliate, had a budget for "a college kid or a drunk," which is why I was allowed to audition for the weekend weather gig in the first place. To be clear, I was a college student, not a drunk. I was never a stand-around-with-a-brewski-chatting-about-sports-with-the-guys kind of guy. Other than the occasional glass of fruit punch at the Rathskeller (our college bar), it would be many years before I started drinking in earnest. By the time I was introduced to some of the finer libations—the Pimm's Cup, the Gatsbyesque gin and tonic, the *where-have-you-been-all-my-life* deliciousness of the Aperol spritz—I was married and had three children.

Dr. O'Donnell, or "Doc" as all the students called him, was an excellent professor but his notoriety around campus came from his second job. His side hustle. Every afternoon, after wrapping up a day of teaching classes, grading papers, and holding office hours, he'd head to the WHEN studios where he'd place a miniature trolley over his head. It covered everything except his eyes, which peeked out of the trolley mask like eerie little globes. His nose, covered by a red bulb, was the trolley's headlight. He strapped a little cowcatcher beneath his chin—and his transformation from distinguished department head to Mr. Trolley of *The Magic Toy Shop* was complete. (In case you aren't familiar, a cowcatcher does not "catch cows" per se. A cowcatcher is actually a metal frame attached to the front of a train to *move aside* cows or any other major obstacles that might be in the way. Imagine what that would look like for just a second.)

Mr. Trolley's voice had the timbre of Goofy with distinct side notes of the Lion from *The Wizard of Oz*. It was not at all how Dr. O'Donnell sounded in class when leading a discussion about communication theory. SUNY Oswego's graphic design teacher, Socrates Sampson (yes, that's his real name), played his jovial sidekick, Eddie Flum Num, and they were joined in song by Merrily and her magic music box, who was played by Marilyn Herr, the station's public affairs director. The trio became very popular, despite the fact that they sang chipper songs that were actually cloaked in darkness. They sang about "teddy bear picnics" and how it's best to not go into the woods, and *dear God if you do, don't go alone*—really, please, everyone should just stay home! Apparently, back in the 1960s and '70s, terror was the way to get children to tune in to a TV show. Doc had been doing this since 1955 and *The Magic Toy Shop* became the most popular local children's television show in history. No one has beat it to this day. Years later Dr. O'Donnell would say, "Al, say what you will, but that F#&king trolley paid for my kids' college."

Andy Brigham, the news director, had asked Mr. Trolley if any of his students might fit the bill. In other words, who could do a decent job of pointing at a weather map on local TV for forty bucks a weekend? O'Donnell tapped me and three lucky others. We were all earnest communications majors. None of us were the sorority-girl-chasing, raging-kegger jock types who would be too busy partying on weekends to show up for the weather forecast. You know . . . nerds. We were all a fairly safe bet. We took turns practicing our weather forecasts, using two large maps made for us by none other than sidekick-extraordinaire Eddie Flum Num himself. We switched back and forth between the map of the United States and a New York State map. We practiced pointing while speaking to the camera, swooping our hands down the map to emphasize low pressure–rain is coming! Resist the allure of suede, people! Then we'd try it again, this time adding our most dazzling smiles. We kept pointing-speaking-smiling until Dr. O'Donnell felt satisfied with our performances. Finally, we each recorded a tape of our forecast for the news director in the studios of Lanigan Hall. Lanigan Hall was a fairly new facility that housed the public radio station. It contained several studios outfitted with various hand-me-down equipment. But for an AV nerd from Queens who had never seen so much equipment in one place, my mind was blown. Tape recorders, microphones, cameras, and more cameras! Up until that point, my media experience was limited to what I did in AV club in high school.

I went to an all-boys Catholic military school, Xavier High School on West Sixteenth Street in Manhattan. Xavier was unique in that we were required to wear military uniforms. And in addition to your typical high school fare there was catechism, and also military science where we learned to execute actual military drills. Once a month we'd head up to the Twenty-Third Street Armory to march around in formation inside a Civil War–era fortress. Yes, it was a Jesuit military academy, so in addition to being able to recite the Hail Mary and Our Father, we would also be prepared in the event New Jersey decided to invade Manhattan via the Hudson River. Bring it on! I was a decent student, but I wasn't the weapon-wielding type. I wasn't about to join the squad drill team and toss around those shiny white practice rifles topped off with bayonets. Besides lacking strength, hand-eye coordination, or any desire to join at all, I had a profound fear of a knife-topped weapon burying itself into my person.

Nope, that was not my thing.

I found my crew underground . . . literally. They would hang in the bowels of our ancient school building, right across from the supply room. The AV club guys were my people and we were pretty tight. Let's face it, who would want to hang with us? Today we would be the internet geeks, running the school website, proficient in coding, video games, and not getting girls. In 1968, it was multimedia rather than social media. Need a film strip to synchronize perfectly with the accompanying record that provides the audio? Consider that handled. Threading the loops for the 16 mm projector? Piece. Of. Cake. We walked the halls of Xavier High School proudly with our heads held high, pushing our rolling carts like tiny nerd bosses. A line from *SpongeBob* the movie pretty much captures our situation. SpongeBob, ever the optimist, tells his dim-witted starfish sidekick, "They're not laughing at us, Patrick. They're laughing next to us."

I don't know who it was that came up with the idea, but we eventually came to the conclusion that a group as close-knit as we were should have its own "hand gesture." It had to be something that would bond us together and represent our solidarity and commitment to serving the audio-visual needs of the school. And this is how we ended up being the one and only AV club that had its own gang sign. Should one AV-cart-pushing geek pass a fellow AV brother in the hallways, we'd look each other directly in the eye and then throw the sign. The thumb and pointer finger would be held upside down, with the index finger from the other hand placed across that, indicating an A–then swiftly turned upright without said finger, to display a V.

It had been years since I was a full-fledged AV club dork, but the reality was that I was still just a college kid, so I was reluctant to get my hopes up about the weekend weather gig. It had been a few weeks since I sent in my audition tape and I hadn't heard anything. Maybe they were going for someone slimmer, less bald, and less black? Did a guy like me even stand a chance? Perhaps they found the perfect drunk? I was about to tell myself to just accept that it wasn't going to happen when Dr. O'Donnell asked to speak to me after class one day. "Roker, I've got some news." Dr. O'Donnell was gathering up his books and papers as he spoke, presumably because he was headed off to his more lucrative job of portraying a trolley. "So, Andy Brigham took a look at your tape and he wants you to do an in-studio audition. And there's one more thing—you'll be doing it with Ron Curtis." Ron Curtis! This is perhaps one of the few times in my life I could genuinely say I was *flummoxed*. As far as Central New York was concerned, Ron Curtis was the Walter Cronkite of Syracuse. In the 1960s and '70s, as the anchorman of the *CBS Evening News*, Walter Cronkite was a media legend, and so universally revered, he was known as "the most trusted man in America." Me, a mere college student, auditioning with *the* Ron Curtis, the most trusted man *in Syracuse*? Born Ron Ezzo, he anglicized his name to Ron Curtis, a practice very common amongst media personalities during that time. People didn't let their ethnicity show—everyone

just wanted to blend. Ron Curtis was a refined guy: Italian, sophisticated, and always dressed impeccably. To this day, I've never forgotten the model of class and style that was Ron Curtis. He always wore a perfectly crisp white shirt whether on the air or just in his office . . . and never, ever would you catch him in colored shirts! I never once saw him with his jacket off.

When I got to WHEN the morning of my audition, I looked around and noticed that I stood out like a sore thumb. WHEN was housed in a midcentury, modern glass-and-stone structure that might as well have been the Guggenheim compared to WSYR, the NBC affiliate's modest, tan brick structure just a block over. But I stood out as much as the building did, for what some would say were all the wrong reasons. I was a young, chunky, black college kid. I was already losing my hair and was wearing a borrowed blazer with flared slacks and a polyester patterned shirt. (I had pulled the whole look together myself!) Who knew that forty years later I would be in that same building cutting promotional spots with their anchor team, plugging *The Today Show*?

I walked across the lobby to reception, the sun shining through the large glass window. Reception sent me upstairs via a midcentury modern staircase, not unlike the one in *The Brady Bunch* family's house. It had the most delicate and useless railing to ever grace a stairway. One wrong step and you'd fall to your death. (How did those six kids survive in that house? Where's the childproofing, Mike and Carol?) When I met Ron Curtis he could not have been nicer, asking me about my major and where I grew up. When I told him I was from New York City, he said that the CBS station in New York wanted him to be their anchor but his entire family was in Syracuse, so he wanted to stay. He actually turned them down! I still think of Ron when an opportunity presents itself–like when I was offered the chance to drive the pace car through the iconic Indianapolis 500 racecourse over Memorial Day weekend one year. The pace car? Me? *The air blowing over my bald head.* But I try to choose my family every time due to Ron's example.

Ron dubbed me "Big Al" right there during the audition. It was a nod to *Rowan & Martin's Laugh-In,* the popular sketch comedy show, and the comedian Alan Sues, who was known as Big Al. I had a nickname! That must mean I've landed the job, I thought walking out of there.

After my audition college life resumed as normal, but I was anxious to find out if I had indeed gotten the job. Of course I wanted the job. What college student wouldn't prefer weekend weatherperson over pizza delivery guy or burger flipper? This was a dream job; it was a chance to do what I wanted to do. But there was also the matter of $500. I had put down a $500 deposit to do a study-abroad program at the BBC in London. I had worked hard, saving every penny I earned working in the dining hall, and what I made working at the SUNY public radio station, WRVO, as well as at WSGO, the local easy-listening station. "Earn Big Money in Broadcasting!" the job advertisement had said, and I earned a whopping $3.50 per hour playing the calming sounds of Mantovani, Percy Faith & His Orchestra, and Andy Williams. Big money indeed. I had never been out of the country in my entire life and all my college friends and I were going on this trip to London. We were going to learn about media at the legendary British Broadcasting Corporation. There'd be fish-and-chips, tea, and I'd finally learn what a crumpet was. Who knows, maybe we'd even catch a polo match. It was London! I pictured myself walking about the streets sporting a deerstalker cap and wearing a mackintosh to keep myself dry, and crying out "The game's afoot!!" Obviously, a jolly good time would be had—but what if I got the job? I couldn't afford to forfeit $500.* Worse—what if I didn't get the job? The mental gymnastics I was doing were exhausting. (A) If I got the job and I didn't go to England, I'd lose my $500 deposit. (B) If I asked for my deposit back but didn't get the job, all of my friends would go to England and have that jolly ole time without me, while I'd be back home delivering pizzas to drunk coeds or operating a deep fryer. (C) I could ask for my deposit

---

*In 1974, $500 was about equal to $2,616.34 considering a cumulative rate of inflation at 423.37 percent, in case you were wondering.

back, and I just might get the job. I decided option C was the most appealing. Yes, I was going with option C. It was with great reluctance that I asked for my deposit back, knowing I would not be traveling to England and visiting the great BBC with my friends, so I threw all my energy into getting that job.

My follow-up campaign began immediately. I called Andy Brigham at WHEN, and I was relentless. The switchboard operator/receptionist got so used to my calling that we became friends. I knew her name was Rosie, and she had heard all about how badly I wanted this job. It got to the point that she would actually recognize my voice.

"WHEN Syracuse," Rosie would say.

"Hi, there, it's Al Roker calling for Mr. Brigham." A pause.

"Oh, hi, Al. He's not in, sweetie, but I'll make sure he gets your message." For those of you too young to remember, a switchboard operator was an actual live human being who answered the phone and connected you to the person you were calling, or took a message. On a piece of paper! This pattern of call, leave word, call, leave word again would continue for the next two weeks. I called the station so often that I had the phone number memorized. One day, to my shock and surprise, Rosie said, "Hold on just one minute, Al."

Behold! A few seconds later this gruff, smoky voice came on the phone and barked out: "Brigham! What?"

YOU LOOK SO MUCH BETTER IN PERSON • 15

I was caught completely off guard. I was like a dog who was so used to chasing a car that he had no idea what to do when he finally caught it. I stammered incoherently, eventually blurting out something about how this was Al Roker and . . . um, had he made a decision about the job? In an exasperated voice and with a big sigh he said, "Roker. Clearly the only way to get you off my ass is to give you this job."

Andy wanted me off his ass! He was giving me the job! He made a comment about seeing me soon and got off the phone as quickly as possible.

While I'd like to think Andy hired me because he saw something in me—a budding and talented weather forecaster, an affable interviewer who would create dazzling interview segments—I know this likely wasn't the case. I got this job for one reason only: I kept my eye on the prize. Once I let the opportunity to study in London go I was determined to get this job. I would make it known I wanted it and I'd show my persistence, all while being charming and polite at the same time. And I wouldn't stop until (a) I got the job or (b) WHEN issued a restraining order against me. Every time I was tempted to give up my campaign, I'd remember that shiny prize: a college job as a weather forecaster. The grand prize represented a lot to me—an actual paying job in the profession I wanted to work in, validation that I was right to give up a chance to study abroad with my friends, and perhaps most important . . .

hope that it didn't ultimately matter that I was a black, overweight kid from Queens. Eventually my focus paid off and I got hired. There's something to be said for keeping your eye on the prize, for knowing what you want and going after it wholeheartedly. To be clear, if they had flat out said, "No way, Roker, we're not hiring you, kid," I would have moved on, but until that opportunity was closed I was going to keep going for it. If you want something badly, keep at it until it's yours or it's no longer an option. Don't stop because you *think* you've tried hard enough and you *believe* it's not going to happen. Don't make those assumptions. Stop when you receive a flat-out NO. If and when that does happen, you can channel all that energy you devoted to seeking your prize to pursuing a different opportunity.

And when you do find yourself actively going after a big prize, know this—the phone is your best tool. To this day I am a passionate believer in the power of a phone call. Pick. Up. The. Phone. A text or an email are a start, but they do not ultimately create a personal connection. It's so easy for someone to choose not to respond to an email or a text. But if you get them on the phone it's unlikely they will refuse to speak to you. A telephone conversation is an actual back-and-forth situation—information can be exchanged and relayed in real time! Mark my words, want to get something done? Pick up that phone. And don't even get me started on the magic that can happen via letter writing. Want to completely blow someone's mind? Write a real letter. Use ink and paper . . . and put the paper in an actual envelope. And put a stamp on it. And mail it!

I was so proud of my follow-up campaign and was still reeling for days from the news that I was about to become an official weatherperson. On TV. I wanted to squeeze this opportunity for everything it had to offer and I wanted to put my best foot forward. But when do I start? How much money will I be making? I gave Andy a quick follow-up call (he was starting to sound like he might regret his decision) to get the particulars. I was going in the following week to learn the ropes—and I was going to start that weekend! This was just at the end of my sophomore year, so I knew I still had so much to learn . . . but one of my immediate concerns was what was I going to wear? I had dutifully returned the borrowed blazer after my audition. The bulk of my wardrobe consisted of flannel plaid shirts and denim overalls. Farmer chic. My dressiest items were a few button-down polyester shirts with gigantic collars, jeans, a pair of flared slacks, and a single extrawide avocado-green tie with mustard-yellow stripes. I couldn't walk around the dorms hustling and searching out blazers to borrow before every newscast. It was time to make an investment in my wardrobe. I went to the finest men's store in downtown Syracuse that I could afford, J. C. Penney.

On my meager budget, I proudly left the store with three suits at $59.99 apiece. But wait, that's not all. Each jacket came with two pairs of pants . . . and a reversible vest. One suit was a polyester faux denim, one dark brown–light brown, and for those days when I needed to feel extra sure about myself, there was a lime green–forest green combo. There wasn't a natural fiber within three miles of these outfits, but according to my calculations these pieces could result in an astounding 120 different combinations.* I was set.

To this day I still enjoy putting together a good outfit. This is due to the late Ron Curtis's influence, and I'm grateful for it. What I choose to put on in the morning is a sign of respect for my craft, and it sends a message about who I am. I might get up at 3:45 A.M. every morning, but I'm still going to take pride in my appearance. Who wants to get their weather forecast from some slob in a wrinkled polo shirt? Who wants to start their day with him? A good crisp shirt suggests that this guy knows what he is talking about!

Unless I am being tossed around by winds in the middle of a hurricane, or maybe covering a Nascar race (or dressed like Fred Flintstone or Oprah Winfrey for Halloween), I am wearing a shirt and tie. When I first laid eyes on Ron Ezzo I knew immediately that I wanted to emulate him. He was stylish but there was an effortlessness to it. He knew exactly what worked for him and he wore suits

---

*That works out to about $1.50 per outfit.

with ease. His wardrobe was classy; Ron looked intelligent, sophisticated, friendly, and approachable, and that's exactly the vibe you want to get from the guy who gives you your evening news. I've played with my style over the years and I'm not afraid to admit I've been inspired by some major style crushes. Paul Feig, who directed the film *Bridesmaids* and the remake of *Ghostbusters,* is a real piece of man candy when it comes to style. That guy knew he wanted to wear a three-piece suit since he was eight! I love that Paul wears well-tailored three-piece suits and is open to bold patterns and crazy colors. His overall look is kind of a throwback to old Hollywood, which is impressive since in Los Angeles anything goes. That unshaven guy wearing the dirty T-shirt in front of you in line at the juice bar? He could very well be directing a movie with a $100 million budget starring Al Pacino. But Paul, he's always dressed to the nines. It's like he's an ultra-thin Alfred Hitchcock. Paul's look has prompted me to try new things—vests, double-breasted jackets . . . but I do draw the line at a top hat. And to all the weekend TV anchors, sportscasters, and weatherpeople . . . wear a tie.

I cringe to think back on those mix-and-match polyester suits, but I've come a long way, in part thanks to my style crushes like Ron and Paul. Having a style crush can be a huge help and I highly encourage it. Whose style really floats your boat? Are you a throwback Kate Spade, Dean Martin, or Beyoncé type? Or maybe ultra-modern is your thing: think Victoria Beckham. What is it about your style crush's look that sets your heart aflutter? Is it whimsy? Speaking of . . . the Rock wears a three-piece suit with a vest and *a lapel.* Now that kills me. Or is it sophistication and clean lines? Is it a sense of mystery? (How does Anna Wintour walk around with sunglasses indoors and not trip over anything?) Crush hard, emulate their style—just don't be afraid to add your own personal touches.

Now that I had the pressing question of wardrobe sorted out, I had to tell my mom the big news. I got back to my dorm room with my new, nearly unlimited wardrobe and dialed my parent's number back in Queens. At that time it was considered long distance from Syracuse and that was expensive, but I wanted to share my news. I knew Mom would be home. The phone rang two times before she answered: "Hello, Roker residence."

"Mom, guess what? I got the job. I'm going to be the weekend weatherperson on channel 5, WHEN up here in Syracuse."

There was a quick pause before she responded with great pride and excitement. "You're going to be on TV? I can't believe it! You said channel 5? What time? I can't wait to watch!"

At that point, in 1974, Mom hadn't had much opportunity to travel, and TV to her meant the three big network channels—ABC, NBC, and CBS—and maybe an occasional venture over to public television. The concept that there were other local stations in other parts of the country did not compute. Television to her was what existed on the set right there in her living room.

"Thanks, Mom, but it's channel 5 in Syracuse. It's not the same channel 5 like you guys have in New York City."

"Al, I know a five is a five." I could hear as her voice shifted from pride to a mixture of disbelief combined with a touch of "don't sass me, I'm your mother." "I'm going to walk over to the TV and turn on channel 5 right now. See! Channel 5 is on now!"

I heard the sound of the local broadcast faintly in the background.

"Mom, I know you have a channel 5 in New York. I'm telling you—it's not the same five. I'm in Syracuse! You're in New York City! The signal from here in upstate doesn't reach down there. They are different channel 5s!"

She persisted with skepticism. "Are you trying to tell me that a five is different in New York City than it is in Syracuse? I didn't go to college, but I certainly know a number five when I see one."

I was making no progress. It would be a losing battle. The score was currently Al–0 and Mom–1.

"I know it's a five, Mom, it's just a different station."

The Abbott and Costello routine could have continued indefinitely; my point wasn't getting across to her. But it was long distance and Mom knew I couldn't afford a big phone bill, so I told her that I loved her and we said goodbye. I carefully put my new supercool jackets, slacks, and vests into the closet I shared with my roommate, still stunned that I had bought work clothes for my new television job as a local weatherperson. I shut the closet door, walked over to my desk, sat down, and opened up a textbook. I was excited for this new chapter of my life. I couldn't wait to see where it would take me, but for now I had to hit the books. I had homework to do.

ALTRUISM #2

If You're Gonna Cry,
Know How to Cry

THE YEAR 1975 was notable for a few reasons: the debut of *Saturday Night Live*, the disappearance of Jimmy Hoffa, Patty Hearst landed on the FBI's Most Wanted list, the Vietnam War came to an end, and Bruce Springsteen released his hit album *Born to Run*. That summer the movie *Jaws* would reign supreme in its popularity and—voila!—movie fans were pummeled by an enormous shark snacking on the beachgoers of Martha's Vineyard; it would instill fear in the hearts of swimmers everywhere. It also inspired the nickname for my hot-tempered resident curmudgeon of a news director, Andy Brigham, a.k.a. "Jaws."

Andy was my first real news director and my first real boss. He was a terrific investigative reporter but a little gruff. Andy was rough around the edges and usually sported a tattered sweater (which might or might not be stained, depending on the day of the week and/or what he ate for lunch), his hair was slick, and his overly loud voice could probably be heard in Canada. I've been known to give a good nickname . . . my nicknames really, really stick. Take veteran NBC News photographer Tony D'Amico. When I got my start at WNBC doing the weekend weather in New York City, Tony was starting out as a desk assistant. A fun-loving Italian guy from Brooklyn, Tony showed up every single Saturday with a bag of warm donuts from his local Italian bakery. So, naturally I started calling him Tony Bag O' Donuts, eventually shortening it to Tony Donuts. Over the years Tony would become one of the best news field camera guys we have at NBC, but everyone still calls him Tony Donuts. I'm very proud of that.

But back to Jaws. Great white sharks are generally really big. The average female shark is fifteen to sixteen feet long and a male can be as long as thirteen feet. The shark in *Jaws* was a whopping twenty-five feet long. Massive. It should come as no surprise then that the mouth of the fictional monster shark would be enormous. Picture the size of an extra-roomy car trunk, big enough to easily accommodate multiple gnawed-up human corpses. While Andy didn't share the shark's proclivity for dining on human flesh, he could really chew a person out. He was positively famous for it. And when it happened, everyone knew it. You could be sitting at your desk hard at work on a story, happily in synch with the buzz of the newsroom—the constant phones ringing, typewriters clacking. (For those of you who don't know what typewriters are, imagine that your keyboard is connected directly to your printer. Every time you hit a key, the key's letter is physically printed on paper by a small piece of metal with that same letter engraved on it. Ask your parents.) Add that sound to the banter between news folk and the perpetual shuffling of papers, when suddenly a hair-raising bellow would cause the entire newsroom to stop cold. It could start with a

simple "God. Damn. It!" or "What in the hell?" But everything would come to a halt and the newsroom would be
overtaken by a foreboding silence. It was like somehow
even the phones knew to stop ringing. We all sat motion-
less waiting to see who would be the next victim of Jaws.
You prayed. Oh, how you prayed the upcoming diatribe
wouldn't be directed at you!

Finally, Jaws would shout out the person's name, breaking the silence. "Rob!! Get over here. Now!"

Rob, or whoever was about to be chewed down to a
pulp, would sheepishly follow Andy back into his office,
letting the door close behind him. The door might as well
have been left wide open because nothing short of a bank
vault could muffle the sound of an epic Andy chew-out.
Another *"God damn it"* would generally be followed up by
a long string of expletives, occasionally punctuated with
an f-bomb to really drive home the point that you had
royally F#&ked up. A number of things could set Andy
off: cheesy copy, bad grammar, the incorrect use of the
word "literally," weak coffee, an unsatisfactory sandwich,
or a missing stapler.

To be clear, Andy also provided guidance, mentorship,
and served as an example of journalistic excellence for me
and countless others. I am forever grateful for everything
he taught me. He wanted us all to do our best and would
do whatever he could to make that happen. But take the
man's stapler? God help you.

Like the majority of America, I too had enjoyed a white-knuckled viewing of the popular fish-themed horror film—sinking down in my seat whenever the familiar *dah-dah dah-dah* sound started . . . increasing in its intensity and fervor as Jaws got closer to its victim. Today that film's ominous attack score is as recognizable as "Jingle Bells" or "Happy Birthday." Who could have imagined that two simple notes played on a tuba could send such a chill up your spine? It was my feeling that the *Jaws* theme song was the universal anthem for incoming danger. So, if I was able to play this song in the newsroom when our very own human Jaws appeared, and just as he was ramping up to chew someone out, I'd actually be providing my colleagues with a sound warning system. A public service if you will. And, PS, it would be really, really funny.

To make my vision a reality I had to physically visit a record store and purchase an actual LP from the movie soundtracks section of the store. The early seventies were basically the equivalent of the Stone Age when it came to procuring music. I flipped past copies of *A Star Is Born* and *Pippin* until I saw the familiar shark head. That was just the beginning. I took the record into the cart room. Back in the seventies, news stories were shot on film and the natural sounds and actual interviews were on the film. Any narration the reporter needed to do or any music that needed to be added was recorded on an audio cartridge, something that looked like an 8-track tape (again, ask your parents). The cart room had a turntable and a mic and a speaker so you could hear what you recorded. And it was right across from Andy's office. So, one day I recorded the theme from *Jaws* onto a 3:30 cart (a three-tiered metal cart on wheels like the kind I used to push around Xavier with pride) and kept it at my desk. A couple of days later, Andy called someone into his office for a royal ass-chewing. Once the victim went in and closed the door behind him, I sprinted to the audio booth with my *Jaws* recording, put it into the cart machine, hit play, and cranked up the volume. The *dah-dah dah-dah* mixed beautifully with the sound of laughter from the newsroom, including my own. What I didn't know was that I had spared Andy's next victim by sacrificing myself.

Suddenly, the door of Andy's office was flung open and he burst out with . . . "What the F#&k is this? Who the F#&k did this?" My colleagues were no longer laughing; in fact they had scattered like cockroaches. There I stood alone, with my finger suspiciously resting on the play button. I was busted. "What the F#&k, Roker? What in the F#&k is wrong with you?" I had witnessed Andy's outbursts on many occasions, but this was next level.

As I looked at Andy, his eyes on fire with rage, his neck stretched out and his face red, I felt something start to happen. I became aware that my bottom lip was quivering involuntarily. My breathing was becoming ragged and I immediately noticed that my eyes were welling up. Was this actually happening? It was happening. I was going to cry. As soon as the first tear ran down my cheek, Andy grabbed me by the arm, surprisingly gently, and led me outside.

By the time we reached the parking lot I was really going at it. I was crying like a kid who had his balloon popped and his ice cream cone thrown to the ground by a malicious clown. At that moment it felt like life would never ever be okay, ever again. I was trying and failing to regain my composure. Then Andy pulled a handkerchief out of his back pocket and handed it to me. I must have hesitated (Andy's hygiene was questionable at times) because he said, "Go ahead, kid, it's clean."

I wiped my eyes and blew my nose, terrified that this moment of kindness was really the calm before a massive storm. I braced myself for whatever was going to come next. "Aw. Shit, Roker. Now, I can't have you crying on me. You're making me break my own goddamn rules! You never make the talent cry!" I continued to try to gain some composure. "But here's the thing," he said, "you know I just can't have you raggin' on me in front of the news team. Ya know what I mean?"

Before I had a chance to apologize for what I now saw was a juvenile stunt, I realized that it was Andy who was comforting me. Even though I had embarrassed him, his focus was on making me feel okay. Contrary to his regular explosions, he was a genuinely nice guy—I knew that—but he was doing it because he had a job to do, and that job was to put on quality news broadcasting. I might have made a jerk move, but Andy knew that helping me collect myself so I could actually do the job was more important than a bruise to his ego. He might have been supremely ticked off—he had given me such a huge opportunity by hiring me when I was only in college! Then I repay him by acting like an idiot. But Andy had the wisdom to focus on the matter at hand: getting the job done. And that meant helping me get my sorry-crying-self in order quick.

Once my breathing returned to normal and my nose stopped running, we had an actual conversation. "So, Roker. Whaddya doing this weekend? Any good plans?"

I was still slightly suspicious about whether there would be a storm so I said sheepishly, "Maybe a movie or something?" I quickly added, "But definitely not *Jaws*." Andy laughed.

"Roker. Seriously, you need to relax. I'm not going to bite you." It was like the conversation had moved from getting my butt reamed to a breeding ground for puns. I laughed, and at that moment realized everything was going to be okay.

There's no denying the fact that you are an actual human being when you experience strong emotions, and we all have our own responses, from shutting down to lashing out, or if you're like me . . . *crying*. Confession: I still cry at work. I'm not just talking about a single tear either, or the slight watery blurb after a heroic story in a segment. I, Al Roker, have ugly-cried. I am four decades into my job so I'm no longer crying about getting in trouble from my boss for pulling a stupid stunt, but sometimes things just get to me and—hello waterworks! If you've suffered the loss of a loved one, emotions can overtake you at the most inopportune and random moments (like on live television in front of the entire nation). Recently we did a segment about someone dying of lung cancer on *Today*, and I could feel it getting to me as I started thinking about my parents. It's almost like knowing you're getting sick—one moment you feel fine, the next you're really regretting that decision to buy discount sushi at the corner deli. It comes on like a punch to the face that you didn't see coming. I started to sniffle and I had to get out of my chair, quick. I made it to the men's room where I really went at it; I had a good five-minute-long sob session. My co-workers were concerned of course, but they kindly gave me my space. I'm a human being with emotions, like all of us (except the one percent of the population who are psychopaths), and sometimes they take over.

Crying in public or at work is a debatable topic. As a workplace crier, a man who has cried and survived more than once, my advice is . . . know how to cry. If you're a sniff or two kind of crier, well, people will likely just think you have allergies, so go for it. Then we have the ugly-cry. If you are a full-out, gasping for breath with ten to fifteen

seconds of silence preceding the big cry, then I highly rec-
ommend you find a safe space in which to cry and com-
pose yourself afterwards. When I emerged from the men's
room after my big cry I simply said, "Wow. Sorry, guys.
That really hit me from out of nowhere." And I got on
with it all. I didn't let it take down the rest of my day. The
good news about this kind of cry is that it tends to be pow-
erful but quick. Like a purge. Being an ugly-crier is nothing to be ashamed of per se, but it is important you know
this style of crying can cause alarm amongst co-workers
and superiors.

Easter Sunday services nearly always pull a cry out of
me, but this cry falls into an entirely different category . . .
the misty cry. There's a hymn my mother always loved,
and I can picture her in my mind standing in church, rais-
ing her arms up as she sang along. This beautiful memory
on this meaningful day makes me cry, and as far as I'm
concerned this is an incredibly reasonable response. I've
embraced this style of crying; it's easy to rebound from.
The misty cry, or what I sometimes call the trigger cry,
is acceptable. It's a genuine expression of human emotion in a dose that is generally enough for colleagues to
handle. It's obvious you're crying, but it's not happening
at such a dramatic level that it causes discomfort to those
around you. With this kind of crying, just let a tear or two
roll, remember that you are an actual human being who
has feelings, then grab a tissue, take a breath, and get on

with it all. But whatever kind of cries you feel coming on, I think it's better to face them.

There's no need to stuff them somewhere down deep where they'll just percolate for days, bursting out of you when you least expect it. It's hard to get comfortable showing your emotions (and rumor has it that this can be harder for men), but if we all got used to it the world would be a better place. It's a few tears! There's no need to panic, people!

When I cried for the first time at work—ugly-cried in front of my boss Andy—I grew up a little bit. First, I learned the very important lesson that not all helpful people present themselves to the world with a candy-apple smile. Sometimes it takes a little work to get to someone's goodness, and it's worth it. As I wiped away my tears that day in the parking lot I understood that I had a job to do, and Andy had a job to do, and while it's true my prank was childish there was no time to dwell on that. We had to face our feelings: mine (terror and massive remorse) and Andy's (Jesus, this kid is a mess and I can't believe I'm listening to him cry in a goddamn parking lot), and move forward. I also fully understood that we have no off switches. Andy, although a yeller, was authentically himself. He was kind but abrupt. Nurturing but not likely to show this side of himself too frequently. I might have been more emotional than he was but I wasn't judged for it. Andy let me be authentically myself too.

Andy and I walked back into the office together. Everyone briefly looked up from their typewriters to note that I was alive with all limbs intact. Sure, I was slightly puffy-eyed from my big cry, but I was ready to move forward. "Go on, kid," Jaws said, "what are you waiting for? You're on in ten!"

ALTRUISM #3

Keep Your Day Job

FOR DECADES, before the local news started, rather than the pithy opening notes that indicated an episode of *Seinfeld* was forthcoming, a public service message would announce: "It's 10:00 P.M. Do you know where your children are?" It almost came off as a warning. *Hey you! Yeah, it's you I'm talkin' to—before you kick back to watch the news with that second martini, I suggest you locate the whereabouts of little Bobby and Rosie. Pronto.*

I had been doing the weather at the local station in Syracuse for two years—long enough to cycle through every combination in my mix-and-match wardrobe—when I got a call about a job from Arthur Albert, the assistant news director at WTTG in Washington, DC.

"Roker. I got a call from a news director friend of mine up there in Syracuse," Albert said, "and he says you're someone I'll want to get a look at."

I was stunned by this information. Someone said I'm a guy to take a look at?! Not to mention that the job was in Washington, DC. That was a major market! It was closer to home too. Mom would be pleased.

I'd eventually learn that his "friend" wasn't recommending me out of some fraternity-style loyalty to a fellow news director, trying to help a young weather guy like me get a leg up. But since I was a popular weatherperson who simply existed in the same market, I was The

Competition. By "recommending" me for another job in a different area, he was actually getting rid of me so his station could thrive in my absence, in my humble opinion.

Adios, Roker! And good luck to you, sir!

WTTG was flying me down for an interview. I was making $12,500 per year in Syracuse,* and I knew a market like DC would pay more—if I could get above twenty g's I would be living large. I was married by then, hoping to buy a condo, maybe a nicer car, and even start a family. Doubling my salary, even if it meant my cost of living would be higher, sounded like a pretty good deal to me.

After an audition and interview with the news director he told me that "the other stations around here might pay more, but with us you'd be on the number one 10:00 P.M. newscast." Number one? Well, that's something! Nope! It wasn't until after I accepted the job and relocated to Washington that I learned this was the number one 10:00 P.M. newscast because it was the only one.

No other station was doing a 10:00 P.M. newscast. The truth was, after just two years as a weatherperson, I wasn't qualified to be in a major market. I was still too wet behind the ears. But this station wasn't willing to pay for someone

---

*That's about $56,672.01 today at a cumulative rate of inflation of 353.4 percent. That's not bad! In retrospect I should have invested in a new wardrobe made of natural fibers, eschewing any colors that were also flavors.

who was ready. In this regard we were very well matched. *And* it was another channel 5, which would be a huge relief to my mother (even though she'd still be unable to watch the broadcast).

I spent the next few months working hard, trying to get my bearings, keeping my head down, but paying attention to everything–trying to do a good job. "It's 10:00 P.M. Did you know the guy who is about to give you the weather report for your daughter's upcoming wedding this weekend just got out of college, doesn't know what he's doing, and until a few months ago thought wearing a lime-green polyester vest on live television was a good idea?"

I had so much to learn, as we all do when we're in the early years of our careers, but I'll admit there is something extra intimidating about learning to do your job on live television. I was determined to get good at this, but I was often plagued by the thought that I just wasn't ready for the job.

It felt like I was sabotaging my career before it had a chance to get started. At this point I had no polish. I was the funny weather guy, but it felt like I was playing a part. I wasn't being the real me. We were only on once a day, compared to my affiliates who did the weather two to three times per day, so it was hard to establish a rhythm. I was coming off as smooth as a three-year-old giving a manicure. Luckily, someone reached out to me who would end up playing a seminal role in my life and career.

One afternoon I was sitting in my office, located in a basement off Wisconsin Avenue, when the phone rang. "Um, hello?" I didn't even answer my own phone with any panache!

A voice boomed on the line: "This Al Roker? How ya doin'? Say, let's have dinner! What are you doin' tonight? Great! Dinner it is! I'll pick you up on Wisconsin outside your station." Click!

I wasn't entirely sure but I thought I had just been invited to dinner by the one and only Willard Scott. When I stepped outside at the appointed time there was Willard, larger than life, sitting in the driver's seat of a fire-engine-red Cadillac convertible that appeared to be only slightly smaller than the *QE II*. Enter one of the biggest personalities I have ever met in my life.

"Come on, son, get in! Time's a' wastin'!" he said. And with that he pulled out from the curb, made a hard U-turn across Wisconsin Avenue, and literally parked across the street in front of an old-school Italian restaurant. I apparently looked confused. Had we just driven across the street? Was this our destination? Was this even a legal parking space? Willard looked at me, still sitting in the car. "What are you waitin' for, kid? A written invitation? Let's eat!" Willard got out of his giant car and walked confidently up to the restaurant. A couple walking past said, "Hey! You're Willard Scott!" Willard winked at them. "Have a great night, folks!" I got out of the car, admittedly starstruck. In

Syracuse people certainly knew who Ron Curtis was, but that was small time in comparison. Willard was a full-on superstar. After greeting Willard with a slap on the back, the maître d' sat us at the best table in the restaurant. But it wouldn't have mattered where we sat. Eating dinner with Willard Scott was like eating dinner with the entire restaurant. He was the definition of gregarious. After our chianti was poured, a lovely young woman approached our table. She didn't say a single word; she just sauntered up next to Willard and planted a big pink kiss right on the top of his bald head. My jaw nearly hit the fine white tablecloth.

People constantly came by and said hello. By the end of the evening, Willard's head bore lipstick kisses in several shades. I can assure you that none of these ladies considered kissing my extra-large forehead (thanks to a receding hairline). There was something about Willard that people just adored.

I remember sitting across from him thinking, He knows who I am? I mean, at the time nobody under the age of seventy-five watched *The Ten O' Clock News* on WTTG. If anyone under seventy-five saw my weather forecast it was because (a) they were visiting the elderly or (b) they were a coroner and accidentally saw the news while removing the remains of someone who had died of old age during the broadcast. I couldn't tell you what we ate that night (though if pressed to guess I'd say I ordered the lasagna), but I knew I'd never forget what Willard said to me. After some back-and-forth banter about my career, occasionally interrupted by a fan dropping by, Willard said, "You mind if I offer you a bit of advice?" I sat forward anxiously. I couldn't believe it—was *the* Willard Scott going to give me advice on how to up my game as a weatherperson? I felt like I was being handed keys to a secret castle. "Yes, please! I'm kind of floundering and I need all the help I can get!" I was all ears, excited to hear Willard's secrets. "Listen. You're at the beginning of your career. You've got to be yourself. It's really important—that's something no one can ever take from you. And trust me here, there will be many opportunities for you, but no matter what—don't quit your day job." Quit my day job? Why the hell would I do that? I felt like I was clinging to my day job like it was the last life preserver on the *Titanic*.

Fast-forward to today, and I'm primarily known for my day job as a co-host and weather forecaster on NBC's *The Today Show*. I'm the guy who gives the national forecast: "California is on fire!" "The Rockies are being pummeled with snow!" I've always suspected that most of America gets up to refill their coffee as soon as they see me, returning to the television just in time to hear their local forecast. And I can't say I blame them. *Never mind what's taking place in Colorado or Florida. Do I need an umbrella or not?* I get it, people just want to know what to expect weatherwise in their neck of the woods. But what most people don't know about me is that I am also the poster boy for West Indian stereotypes. I'm not talking about curry chicken and Bob Marley dreadlocks if you're thinking that Roker is as bald as a cue ball. A true island *mon* has multiple jobs, fingers in many pots—oxtail stew all over the place! The last time I counted I had five jobs, and many of them are at NBC. I'm the weatherperson at *The Today Show*, I co-host the third hour of *Today* (sometimes I do a fourth hour), I do NBC Nightly News when there's a big weather situation brewing. I'm the guy who gets to use a pair of giant scissors to cut the ribbon at the Macy's Thanksgiving Day parade, and they also shove me out into the freezing cold to host the Rockefeller Center Christmas tree lighting ceremony every year (although they don't let me actually plug in the tree). I have my own production company, Al Roker Entertainment, which produces TV shows for cable companies, broadcast networks, and branded content for major corporations—and, PS, *we're bicoastal.* Actually . . . add writing this book to the list and that makes eight, add the times when I've played Old Joe in the Broadway hit musical *The Waitress,* even though I can't actually sing, and that's nine! (I *can* talk on pitch!) As great as all my side hustles are, I've never considered leaving my day job . . . and I'm going on forty years and running.

I'd come to learn that Willard knew exactly what he was talking about. While Willard Scott is the quintessential broadcaster, he's worn many hats (technically he's worn many wigs, which he has always admitted to, but that's not how the saying goes). In addition to being a weatherperson, Willard has been an actor, radio personality, comedian, and clown. I'm not talking about some run-of-the-mill, balloon-animal-twisting, birthday party clown either. Willard was *the clown*. A.k.a. Bozo, the world's first syndicated clown. Bozo set the standard for clowns everywhere, and that bar was raised high. We all know that clowns are terrifying and I believe we have Bozo to thank for that. The way his flaming-red hair projected nearly twelve inches from each side of his head, the mouth that took up nearly half of his face, the unnaturally arched eyebrows. The overall vibe Bozo gave off wasn't all happy parades and cotton candy—it was more like *something sinister is afoot here. Run while you can, everyone!*

A few years later, Willard swapped out his Bozo costume when he became the first-ever Ronald McDonald. The story goes that the Washington, DC–area McDonald's wanted a character to sell hamburgers. Willard, working at WRC, modified his Bozo costume and helped come up with the Ronald McDonald we all know and love/fear today. It's a tribute to Willard that his kindness and humanity would transcend a potentially scary character. Of course, Jack in the Box and the Burger King aren't exactly warm and fuzzy either. Ultimately, Willard's enthusiastic and genuinely warm portrayal of Ronald McDonald paved the way for billions of hamburgers to be served. While Willard had great success with clowning (yes, I said that), his work on the radio show *Joy Boys*, and on NASA's weekly space-story program (among other countless things), news broadcasting was his day job, and he was never going to quit the gig that kept the lights on.

I've got like nine jobs, and human sleep consumption should be six to eight hours! The good news is I get to do a lot of different things every day—some that I love, some that I'm good at, and some that I didn't even know I was capable of doing . . . like "singing." I live a well-rounded, exciting life at work and after work. And it isn't because I'm Al Roker on *The Today Show;* it's because of being open to new opportunities. That's the secret ingredient in my career curry. It's been what's kept me going and kept me happy for four decades. So, while you're working the nine-to-five job, don't feel like that's all life will serve you. Keep life interesting—explore ALL your talents and then some, not just the ones you use at work! Maybe you're good at cooking. Line dancing. Karate. Keep moving and growing . . . but keep that damn job. Doing multiple things keeps work fun—and life is more fun when you're not handing over all your money to the landlord.

Willard Scott would become like a second father to me, and that would be the first of many of our meals together, but I couldn't imagine a scenario where I would consider giving up my day job. I'm the son of a Jamaican woman and Bahamian man—you have as many jobs as possible! But as I progressed through my career, explored my interests, and encountered different opportunities, I realized how priceless this advice really was. Weather is my base, and will always be my base. (They will have to drag me screaming out of Studio 1-A someday. That should make for some excellent television.) As you go through life exploring different pursuits and hobbies, I hope you'll find them wonderful, meaningful, eye opening, thrilling even, but for God's sake don't quit that day job! Having a solid base makes it much easier to handle all the ups and downs of life, as well as the challenges those fun side hustles just might throw your way. Live a big life. Push your limits, but take it from a weatherperson/parade host/production guy/master of the cameo appearance/occasional author—keep the day job.

ALTRUISM #4

*Know the Cards and
Play Your Best Hand*

SEVEN MONTHS into my job in Washington, DC, I started to think, I'm getting the hang of all of this. I was hanging out with Willard Scott, for God's sake! Surely some of his expertise would rub off on me? The green behind my ears was no longer visible from blocks away; it was finally starting to fade and I was becoming more confident on the air. Just a few months in, I even successfully reported my first non-weather-hard-hitting news story. "On March 9, 1977, a gunman stormed the B'nai B'rith International headquarters. One hundred and forty-nine people were trapped, including the mayor of DC and Marion Barry who was a council member then. Maurice Williams, a twenty-four-year-old journalist was shot, a security guard named Mack Cantrell was shot and later died from his injuries," said news anchor Al Roker!

This was a huge, breaking story and everyone in the newsroom was out covering some part of it. The entire city was in a state of chaos. When Hal, the news director, got word that Marion Barry had been hit by a stray bullet and was being evacuated and taken to a local hospital, he needed someone there to cover it. Immediately. He looked around the newsroom, his eyes landing on me, the only person left in the entire office. "Roker. Get to the hospital where they're bringing Barry. Now."

My initial reaction to this order was *Uh, what?* Cover a breaking story? Me? But I'm a creature of the studio! My comfort zone was inarguably stories of a lighter nature. Need someone to report on whether or not the giant pandas Ling-Ling and Hsing-Hsing are doing the horizontal panda hulu? I'm your man. Someone needs to cover the tour of the Lincoln Memorial's basement? Sign me up!

"What are you waiting for, Roker?" yelled the news director. "A call from the president? Go!"

That's how I found myself on the back of our courier's motorcycle hanging on for dear life, zigzagging in and out of the thick DC traffic, with no helmet. We were headed for the hospital at breakneck speed. Once we got there, I awkwardly disembarked from the courier's death machine and staggered over to join in with the crowd of reporters. The doctor gave a quick press conference, and I actually managed to ask a coherent question: "Can you tell us anything about Marion Barry's condition?"

Still dizzy and a little nauseous, I was handed the footage I needed by the cameraman, climbed back onto the death bike, and made it back to the studio uninjured, just in time to run the story.

My first foray out of the studio to cover a breaking news story qualified as a success.

So, it was a bit of a surprise when the news director called me into his office and asked me to sit down a few weeks later. He got straight to the point: "Roker. Listen.

I don't think this is working out. I don't want you on the weather anymore."

Excuse me, what did you just say? This news was a punch to the gut. I thought I had done a good job. I thought I had just found my stride. I thought I was on my way to Willard-style stardom. What were the words coming out of his mouth? The days of me being the young kid crying at work in a polyester suit were over. More importantly, I had started to develop a real love for my job. I wanted to do the weather. As far as I'm concerned, weather is the ultimate sweet spot of news broadcasting. Everyone is interested. The weather cuts across every socioeconomic and racial line. No one has ever said, "Thanks for telling me that the blizzard headed our way is bringing twelve to fourteen inches of heavy snow, blustering winds, thundersnow, and hail the size of squirrels, but the weather just doesn't apply to me!" It doesn't matter who you are; if it's raining, you are going to get wet. But it seemed Hal had other plans for me. "Roker, I think you're talented though. I want to move you over to reviewing TV and movies." Me, a movie critic? Was this a good time to mention my favorite things to watch in my rare spare time were old Looney Tunes cartoons? Maybe a Laurel and Hardy flick if it was showing on a Sunday afternoon?

"Spend the weekend thinking about it, and let me know your decision on Monday," he said, guiding me out of his office.

This was the first time that someone flat-out told me they didn't think I was as good as I thought I was. Is weather not what I'm meant to do? If not this, what? Sure, it was possible I wasn't as good as I thought I was, but in my heart I knew I had been working hard. I knew I had more potential, and forecasting the weather was what I wanted to do. I didn't need to spend too much time thinking about it that weekend. I would have to be ready to roll with whatever was next, even if that meant leaving Washington, DC, and finding a new weather gig. I was ready to play my hand, and that meant being ready for whatever cards I was dealt.

I woke up on Monday ready to tell Hal I didn't want to be the TV and film critic. I was nervous and knew it could cost me my job, but it was the right decision for me. When I walked into the office, my stomach in knots, I noticed a hushed atmosphere. The usual noises of the newsroom had been muted. Something was going on. "Hey, Roker! Did you hear the news?"

"What news?" I asked.

"Our news director got fired over the weekend! He had to clear out his desk and everything!"

Am I hearing right? Hal is gone? I headed down into the basement to my desk. I sat down and looked around. While the past few months had been marked by challenges and plenty of insecurity, there had been some successes

too. So I didn't have a five-year plan. I didn't know exactly what the world had in store for me in the career department, but I was positive about one thing: I hadn't gotten anywhere close to being able to do what I believed I could do with the weather. I knew there was so much more for me to learn. I could be so much better. Now I still had a chance to make that happen.

I STUCK TO MY GUNS, and in this case I got lucky (perhaps freakishly so; I had no idea Hal was going to get fired), but walking into the office that day I felt ready for anything, even if that meant clearing out my desk and walking out of the building in shame. Sticking to your guns certainly means looking at the big picture and making the best choice in a given situation, but it doesn't end there. If you're going to play a hand, you've got to be prepared to play that hand. I walked into the office that Monday ready to put my cards on the table; I could have lost my job that very day or things could have remained status quo. The one scenario I wasn't okay with was being a television and movie critic—that's not who I was. It would have felt terrible to lose my job, but I wasn't going to *not* take the risk. It was my career, my livelihood, and my dream—and what's more important than that? I'm not telling you to take huge risks with your job (my God, I don't even play poker!), but when faced with a situation that requires a difficult choice, play the hand that's right for you.

ALTRUISM #5

*You Encounter
More Personalities
Than People*

ONG BEFORE he was known as "the daddy of the DNA test," Maury Povich and I both worked at that same humble news station in Washington, DC. Maury was one of two big names around the office—Maury and another journalist named Pat Mitchell both hosted a daily *Meet the Press*–style news show called *Panorama*. *Panorama* was incredibly influential. But while it was the go-to show that all Washington insiders watched, the ratings were never great. It would be a few years before Maury stumbled on to the recipe for a super successful talk show: babies of unknown origin and the catchphrase "You are not the father!"

During a morning chat around the office water cooler, I learned that Pat and Maury shared the same agent in New York City. *An agent. Wow.* Should I hire someone who can seek out new opportunities for me and negotiate my salary? Are agents able to add exciting bonus items into contracts like free BBQ lunches on Fridays? I was agent-curious.

On one of my trips up to New York City to visit my parents, I set up a meeting with Maury and Pat's agent, Alfred Geller. Short, balding, with a paunch, he was a giant in the television news and representation business. An attorney by training, he was one of those old-school guys who sat behind a big messy desk with an overflowing ashtray in a wood-paneled office. He was soft spoken, until

his voice exploded when barking out orders to his belea-
guered, ever-changing cast of secretaries.

Nancy! Where's my overcoat? I got a meeting uptown
in ten!

Joan! This coffee is lousy, get me the sugar!

Alfred told me to sit down, gesturing to the chair across
from his desk. "So. Maury and Pat said I should consider
you." I felt slightly self-conscious, like I was a show pony and
not a weatherperson. Was I supposed to perform a dance?
Should I have worn some sort of jaunty hat? Alfred started
to tell me about how he operated. "Those other guys, the
other agents in town, they're just going to throw your tape
around to see if it sticks anywhere. I'm not going to do
that." Alfred explained with sincerity that he remained a
real student of the business despite his long career. He
wasn't lacking in the charisma department. He kept a
drama coach on staff named Jerry Krone who worked directly with the clients. Alfred cared about how his clients
talked, looked, read from the prompter, and conducted interviews. His method was to tape clients doing a broadcast
and give them a critique. I was impressed. Maybe he could
help sharpen up my skills, I thought. I wanted to get better
at my craft. "I like you, kid, and we'll see what we can do,"
he said. "But I've got to be honest with you. I have no idea
if I can do anything with you at all." Oh.

And with that, we shook hands—a real gentleman's
agreement! I left the office feeling excited. "Yes, I have an

agent!" I tried to ignore Alfred's postscript, that he wasn't sure he could do a thing with me.

Just a few weeks after our meeting I was surprised to get a call from Alfred.

"Roker? Listen. I got word that the weather guy at WKYC—that's in Cleveland, alright? Anyways, I got word that this guy is a complete disaster. Disaster! You hear me?" Alfred emphasized "disaster" to a great degree. I mean how much of a disaster can a weatherperson actually be? "So. I told them I've got the perfect guy for them. Roker, they want you there yesterday!"

I was smiling in the midst of his disaster story. Cleveland was a major market and this gig wasn't for a *weekend* weatherperson—I'd be THE REGULAR, EVERY DAY OF THE WEEK, THREE TIMES PER DAY WEATHER GUY. But why me? Did every other weatherperson in the nation already turn down this job for some unforeseen reason? Or was Alfred just a great agent? For whatever reason they wanted me, I was going to be excited about the opportunity.

Ah, Cleveland. Today this fine specimen of a midwestern city is home to the illustrious Rock and Roll Hall of Fame. And let's not forget the little house on West Eleventh Street where Ralphie nearly shot his eye out with a Red Ryder BB gun in *A Christmas Story*. But I was lured to Cleveland to be the weekday weather guy at WKYC-TV in 1978, long before the city honored rock and roll legends and provided the setting for classic Christmas films. I didn't know a single thing about Cleveland. I headed to the library with nerd gusto! Before the word "library" conjured up images of dusty books and some old guy with a cane reading the free newspaper, the library was the ultimate source for information. In other words, your local public library was basically Google. As a native New Yorker, I wanted to know a little bit more about what I'd be getting myself into if I relocated to Ohio. What I discovered didn't exactly make me want to run home and pack my bags. Cleveland was once a major manufacturing hub but had fallen on hard times, and the Cuyahoga River that runs through the city was completely polluted as a result. According to what I read, the river had caught on fire thirteen times. Thirteen times! I do weather. I'm not a scientist per se. But I knew something was very, very wrong if a body of fresh water was bursting into flames.

I also learned a few interesting tidbits about one of the recent mayors and his wife. Ask anyone who grew up in Cleveland what Ralph Perk accomplished during his tenure as mayor and I guarantee you they will say, "I have no idea what he did, but I do know he once set his hair on fire." During a ribbon-cutting ceremony at a factory in 1972, a spark from a blowtorch landed on his hair. His pompadour hairstyle was apparently laden with product, and it promptly burst into flames. What's with Cleveland

and flames!!! Luckily the fire was put out immediately, and while thankfully the mayor wasn't hurt, his legacy was etched in stone that day.

And his wife, Lucille? Apparently, bowling was really her thing. When she received an invitation to attend a steak dinner with President Nixon and his wife, Pat, at the White House, she famously declined because the dinner was taking place on her bowling night.

Was I ready to take a job in a city that had a history of weird fires *and* tons of racial strife? Like many parts of America, poverty and racism fueled riots in Cleveland in the late 1960s and into the 1970s. Did I think they were ready for a black, overweight, balding, eye-glass-wearing New Yorker? Did I know how to bowl? No, no, and not so well. But did I accept the job? Hell yeah!

Over the years I have flown into New York City countless times, and I still get a thrill from seeing the expanse of Manhattan below me. I look at the lights and inspiring skyscrapers and think, I love living here. It feels like flying into a wondrous land where anything is possible. I'll just say my experience flying into Cleveland in the mid-1970s felt a bit different.* I saw smoke, and more smoke,

---

*If you're thinking, Wow. Roker is really ragging on Cleveland. What a jerk! Spoiler alert. I loved my time there. It's a terrific city! And the river no longer bursts into flames, which is a notable improvement.

followed by . . . smoke. There was a landscape of steel mills and auto plants going at full tilt. What in the hell kind of hell is this? I thought. While it would be an exaggeration to say the flames shooting out of the smokestacks resembled the river of fire and blood from Dante's *Inferno*, it did cross my mind.

When I got off the plane, I was immediately confronted by news headlines stating that the city was now bankrupt. Under the leadership of thirty-one-year-old Mayor Dennis Kucinich, a.k.a. "the boy wonder mayor of Cleveland" (his other nickname was "Dennis the Menace"), apparently the city had defaulted on $15.5 million in loans from local banks. People were up and leaving the city. I stopped to look around the airport. Was everyone leaving while I was coming in? As I stood with my suitcase looking up at the television screens, ready for my new job and life to begin, TV anchors shouted back at me that businesses were relocating, and there weren't enough residents left to actually pay the taxes. Add this to the over $30 million of debt the city already owed. In my head I was screaming, Whoa. This is one helluva mess I've stepped into! Had I made the right decision? Part of me wanted to turn on my heels and head back to DC immediately. Nothing says "Welcome to your new home" like learning the city you've just moved to is totally broke. Broke, racist, and on fire—these were the circumstances under which my tenure at NBC began.*

WHEN I ARRIVED at the WKYC offices on my first day, I was delighted that the newsroom had one thing we didn't have back in Washington, DC . . . *windows*. In DC we had all been stuffed out of sight down in the basement, and as a weatherperson I found this jarring. Of course the radar can tell us if some bad weather is brewing. However, when I'm about to announce the weather to my local people I prefer to have seen that weather with my own eyes. There's nothing quite like broadcasting to the entire community that it's snowing—only to find out that actually there was no snow, just a doggone double rainbow. Frankly, it's embarrassing. Other than being able to see the light of day—a true gift—the newsroom had the same familiar metal desks, lined up in rows. I smiled as I heard that beautiful newsroom noise: typewriters, phones,

---

*WKYC-TV in Cleveland was actually owned by NBC, so I made sure those years counted towards a big anniversary recently at *The Today Show*. Believe me, I had my eyes on the prize . . . a bouquet made out of bacon. NBC doesn't just give those out for any old anniversary.

papers being shuffled, and the occasional curse word. I instantly felt more comfortable.

As I was getting situated at my desk, deciding which drawer would hold my lunch, and where I'd place my pen holder and paper clips, I noticed the guy at the adjacent desk, eating a ham sandwich and reading a newspaper. "Hi there. You the new kid? I'm John Herrington." I introduced myself, glad that the folks seemed friendly thus far when John said, "Wanna see something weird?" *Did I want to see something weird?* Truthfully, no, it was only my first day! I hadn't even located the men's room! But I didn't want anyone thinking the new weather guy was a poor sport so I said, "Sure, yeah. Great." Keep in mind this was the seventies, a decade dominated by mustaches, hairy chests, scotch, an occasional gold chain . . . *and toupees.* John lifted his toupee off his head while simultaneously opening his mouth to display a hunk of chewed-up ham sandwich. He popped his hair back on his head, closed his mouth, and said, "That's the best you'll see!" He laughed, his mouth still full, and went back to his newspaper. Well, so far Cleveland is definitely not boring, I thought.

Despite my initial fears, my adjustment from New Yorker to midwesterner went smoothly. My wife and I lived in a real house—a nice one, on a charming block in Shaker Heights that could actually be described as *picturesque.* For the first time we actually had a garage! You know you're moving up in the world when street parking is no longer part of your daily routine. Our condo in Washington, DC, was a closet compared to our three-bedroom ranch.

My new news family made sure we felt at home too. There were frequent invitations to dinners at each other's homes, where I quickly got to know my new colleagues. We usually went for cocktails after the eleven o'clock Friday night news. One night we bravely ventured out to a crazy new Japanese restaurant that specialized in . . . wait for it . . . raw fish! Nothing bonds people like experiencing sushi together for the first time. It was like those commercials you see for your local networks, the news crew palling around with each other, slapping one another on the back in a jovial manner. That's how life at Action 3 News really was.

I was getting out into the community too, getting the hang of my new city. I was doing broadcasts from the zoo or one of the many festivals that popped up along the shore of Lake Erie. With each broadcast I was growing more confident. By sheer volume of broadcasts alone I was improving. For the first time ever, I was officially part of a big-market news family: WKYC Action 3 News team of Doug Adair, Mona Scott, Amanda Arnold, Dave Patterson, Joe Pellegrino, and AL ROKER! I was Brick Tamland to Ron Burgundy, or Gordon Howard to Ted Baxter–I was no longer just the weekend weather guy.

While I missed dinners with Willard and the lipsticked canvas of his bald head, there was no shortage of big personalities to keep me on my toes in Cleveland. As a newbie to the Buckeye State, I had a lot to learn about the area and its rich history. I was working on a story and tossed out a question to John, his toupee slightly askew, about the polluted rivers. "Roker, how the hell would I know when the river burned? Why don't you ask the Polish Leprechaun?" *The who?* Was "Polish Leprechaun" a code word for the encyclopedia? Did miniature enchanted creatures actually exist in the Midwest?? But weren't leprechauns always Irish? "Yeah, the Polish Leprechaun—you know, Mike Rehosick, he's at the assignment desk."

Our assignment desk was an elevated, three-sided glass enclosure in the middle of the newsroom. I walked over and found an impossibly short guy sitting at one of the desks. He was bald except for a white fringe that wrapped around his head like icing. His kelly-green polyester slacks were topped off with an enormous white belt, and his white shoes were so shiny it's like they had the power to glamour you. I was transfixed, and apparently Mike knew it. "Yeah, they're terrific shoes, right?" Mike positively beamed with pride, rocking back and forth from foot to shining foot. How much time did he spend polishing those babies? Then he added, "I transition to white right after Memorial Day. So, you had a question?" Mike answered my question, and dozens more during my tenure in Cleveland. Mike was incredible—he was a walking, talking, living archive of any story that had happened in Cleveland over the past thirty years (he wasn't a leprechaun but he might as well have been magic). Facts, history, colorful anecdotes, and stories about local people—Mike knew them all. His passion for the city and wealth of knowledge made all of our stories better. And his white belt and shoes were always a welcome sign that spring had arrived!

Doug Adair was our anchor, and he was basically the Walker Cronkite *of Cleveland*. While Doug was short, with salt-and-pepper hair that trended more towards the salt, a Ron Burgundy comparison would not be out of order. Doug had a big personality. A successful broadcast would have included some ad-libbing for sure, and Doug's gregarious personality easily connected him to his viewers. He did, however, like to toss out a few occasional surprises for the rest of us.

Like many news broadcasts, at WKYC we generally liked to wrap up the show with a light-hearted, feel-good moment to follow up any depressing news. Today it's viral videos with millions of views—look at this adorable video of a toddler bonding with a puppy; they're not the same species but they're like brothers! Or maybe a pig that paints. I actually enjoy the quirky news pieces. I've covered everything from stud penguins being brought into the Bronx Zoo to the artistry of manhole covers, the life of sewer workers, and hot air balloon races in rural Ohio. These pieces are meant to entertain and give you a boost. It's not in-depth investigative reporting—we're not talking about Woodward and Bernstein exposing the Watergate break-in here. Yet Doug would ask these crazy follow-up questions. "Thank you for reporting this delightfully charming piece about shelter dogs being adopted for Valentine's Day, Al. Say, how long does it take to train a dalmatian to fetch a newspaper?"

"I'm not quite sure, Doug." Nervous chuckle. Chuckle.

"Hey, but, Al, how about a pipe and a pair of slippers? Which breed of dog has the worst breath? Is it hard to get one of those tiny sweaters on a German shepherd? Why do dogs bark anyway?"

No topic was safe from the inquisitive Doug Adair. Sometimes we'd try to preempt the awkwardness, laying things on the line before that red light went on to indicate we were on the air. "Doug, I don't have any additional information at all about the wonders of donut-hole manufacturing. So, don't ask me any follow-up questions about it, okay?" As soon as you'd complete the piece, Doug would turn to you and say something along the lines of "Tell me every single thing about the thing you just asked me not to ask about."

I suspected he enjoyed watching us all squirm.

Doug had rattled us all at one time or another, but I began to view his questioning as a somewhat strange (and maybe a little annoying) personality quirk. I don't know why he did this (torture is the most reasonable conclusion), but I understood that he wouldn't stop doing it no matter how nicely we asked—or how mad we got. Doug was who he was, and while he had some very fine traits as a reporter, this quirk of his was just part of the package.

Some of my colleagues would get a little fussy about it, but unless you are a hermit who makes a living whittling kazoos in a remote cabin, you will have to deal with other people. You can't be sidetracked by people who are different from you, or expect them to change or bend to a style you're comfortable with. Being able to deal with different personality types is a secret weapon for success in any area of life, and I was fortunate to learn this lesson at the very first job I had as a kid.

After completing a day of school, I'd walk out the back door of Xavier High School right into an old loft factory building that was the home to A to Z Vending, where I worked. Before every office in Manhattan had a Keurig or Nespresso, and unlimited organic-#glutenfree-vegan-ethically-sourced snacks, you simply had a vending machine and a commercial coffee machine. The vending machine housed all manner of deliciousness, from Lorna Doones and Oreos to Lay's potato chips and those weird crackers filled with neon-orange "cheese." Your average commercial coffeepot was about the size of a witch's cauldron. You could fit four or five toddlers inside it. Easily. A to Z Vending was the source of snacks, coffee, and tea for offices all over New York City. As an overweight, prediabetic kid I had hit the after-school job jackpot. I was surrounded by a mountain of snack foods at all times. While my main responsibility was to fill boxes with the appropriate snacks for the delivery guys, it also fell to me to discard any broken crackers or cookies since they could not be resold. Of course I discarded them directly into my mouth.

My two bosses were Morris and Benjamin Stein, brothers and the owners of A to Z Vending, whom I secretly referred to as the Abbott and Costello of vending. And I don't mean that they were doing comedy routines on the side. Morris was tall and slender and sported a thin mustache. Benjamin, his opposite in every way, was squat and balding. Morris, overall, was an energetic, enthusiastic kind of guy. The idea of a new snack food truly got him excited. I can only imagine how he would love the bacon-BBQ-flavored cheese Whisps I like to snack on today—a chip made out of cheese? Imagine! His opposite, Benjamin, while a nice guy was also a bit of a naysayer. He tended to become overly concerned with things like the logistics of snack transportation or the rising costs of coffee filters.

One day Morris says, "Hey, Al, come back in the storeroom with me for a minute. I want to show you something." While today such a request should send any kid running for the hills, Morris legitimately wanted to show me a new snacking marvel. New snacks aren't exactly invented every day, people!

Morris walked me over to a section of the storeroom where there were boxes stacked upon boxes. He reached in, pulled out a package, ripped it open, and handed me something that looked like a pale, dried-out turd. "Go ahead, kid. Give it a try."

I popped something that felt like a rock into my mouth. Its flavor profile did suggest it might be a cousin to the Frito, but the texture was more titanium than corn chip. "They're good," I mumbled, hoping this lump in my mouth would eventually dissolve into something I could chew.

"What you've got in your mouth right now, Al, is the future of vending!" Morris gestured that we look all around us, where I noticed the neatly stacked boxes were all labeled "Cornnuts." "These things can't break, they'll last forever. I gotta get the guys to push the cornnuts!"

I left the storeroom to continue my work. I was packing Milky Ways, 3 Musketeers, and pretzels into boxes when I ran into Benjamin. "How's it going, kid?"

I mumbled a quick "Good," my mouth completely dried out by the salt-laden piece of concrete still sitting in there, completely unchanged in its composition.

"What's that, kid? Hey. Wait a minute, don't tell me you're eating some of those corn nuts! Did Morris give you that? That meshuggener brother of mine with the corn nuts! People are going to break their damn teeth on those things! They're inedible! You know what's going to happen, don't you, Roker? People will break their teeth! Expensive dental work will be required! We're going to get our asses sued, that's what."

Dealing with these two was a little bit like being the ball boy in a tennis match. I had to watch carefully, know when to move and when to just stay out of the way. Morris and Benjamin were as different as they came, and even though it was just an after-school job, I saw how much easier life could be if you let people just be who they are.

It's not always an easy thing to do, but sometimes it's not about taking sides or knowing who is right or wrong. Even when you're the one who's right. Sometimes it's about getting your job done, and that means not being sidetracked when you work with people who have different approaches, philosophies, and communication styles. You can't expect everyone to change or bend to a style you're comfortable with. And, to be clear, you won't always be comfortable (I never did learn which breed of dog had the worst breath, by the way). But sometimes a short bald man with a giant white belt gives you just the perfect tidbit of information that makes your story shine brighter than his shoes, and you couldn't be happier you get to work with such a person.

ALTRUISM #6

A Spoonful of Humor
Helps Everything
Go Down

THE STUDIO FOR WKYC was located in downtown Cleveland. There was an older, black homeless man who was known to hang around the
area. He had become a bit of a fixture. We'd usually see
him coming and going as we walked to our cars in the
parking garage after the last broadcast. Apparently, one
night this gentleman took a rolled-up newspaper and
swatted Doug in the back of the head. While it's under-
standable that no one wants to be swatted in the back of
the head with anything, the retelling of this story the next
day was quite different. We're in the middle of a broadcast,
about to go to the weather. Mona, Doug's co-anchor (and
wife) was about to introduce me when Doug stopped her.
"Mona, before we go on—Al, I don't know if you heard, but
last night after the eleven o'clock news one of your people
attacked me."

What!!!

I couldn't believe it, and sort of wanted a second to pick
my jaw up from the floor, but we were on air. What Doug
said was incredibly wrong and obviously racist, and I knew
I had to respond to it. Time seemed to slow to a crawl. Do
I respond with outrage and castigate a Cleveland broadcasting legend on the air? Do I ignore the comment and
launch into the forecast? I looked at him and said matter-
of-factly: "Doug, why would a weatherman attack you?"

And then I went ahead and did my forecast. My heart was pounding while I described the upcoming five-day forecast. I was on autopilot, just trying to get through it, wondering what the reaction of our viewers and management was going to be.

Needless to say, the station switchboard lit up. People were furious. They were overwhelmingly outraged by what Doug said. Management decided to suspend and ultimately demote Doug. Thankfully for Doug this was pre–social media, so he wasn't castigated and completely chewed up and obliterated nationwide. Doug and his wife, Mona Scott, ultimately left the station for greener news pastures in Columbus, Ohio, where they had a long career.

Doug's comment was blatantly racist, and speaking out about injustice or racism can be handled in different ways. I chose to defend myself with humor. Sometimes I've had to do it more directly but I think context, intent, and history can guide you in your responses to such ridiculous commentary. Does every comment need a scorched-earth policy? No. But can it be ignored? No. The bottom line is you are not a mini United Nations in charge of policing the behavior of others. People, even racists, are who they are going to be. You have to be who you are and move forward.

I hadn't experienced any blatant discrimination or racism at work until the moment Doug Adair was smacked in the head by a newspaper-wielding homeless man. By the time I left for college my father had moved up the ladder from bus driver to dispatcher to management, and the challenges he faced along his journey prompted him to leave me with this advice: "Al—you're a black kid. You will have to work twice as hard and be twice as good as the kid next to you. It's a fact, that's just the way it is." I never forgot that advice and I still share this same advice with young black people. It remains an unfortunate truth.

When I was first hired in Syracuse, the station management was so worried there would be a backlash about a black weatherperson being on TV that they hired security and extra manpower to answer the phones. (Apparently they were expecting lots of phone calls from outraged viewers. A black man doing the weather! How *dare* you.) Turned out, none of it was necessary. There were no riots in the streets demanding my removal. In fact, there wasn't a single phone call about that new black guy on the show. No one seemed to care that it was a black man telling them the high and low temperatures.

When I got to Cleveland there still weren't many non-white faces doing the weather. There were Jim Tilman in Chicago and Spencer Christian in New York. June Bacon-Bercey was the first female TV meteorologist in the 1970s. The number of black people doing the weather didn't even fill up a single hand. But I truly believed that if anything was going to hold me back it was my weight. While I had been heavy my entire life, I was now crossing the bridge from chubby into *very* overweight. Aside from being black, I did not meet the aesthetic requirements for someone who made their living on TV. The people who give you your news are supposed to be svelte. No one wants to get their weather report from a guy so big he's sweating bullets as he's pointing out the path of an incoming storm. When it came to my challenges, weight trumped race. Black anchors like Matt Robinson, Bernard Shaw, Jim Vance, and Carl Stokes had it harder; they were presenting the news. The hard-news guys suffered more discrimination because they were in positions of authority—they were gatekeepers of information. I was presenting the weather; this position just didn't have the same level of scrutiny. It felt like I was given a pass as the keeper of weather . . . because, once again, people just want to know if it's going to get chilly enough that they need a cardigan.

OVERALL, ALL WENT WELL in Cleveland. Action 3 News was rising in the ratings. We had moved from third place to second. But I did hope to go back to New York someday. The pinnacle of success in the local news business was to be in the number one market, and that meant the Big Apple. And the delicious candy coating on that apple? It was my hometown.

To satiate my hunger for all things New York City, I subscribed to *New York* magazine. It was a weekly dose of the city and the world I missed. Since I did the five, six, and eleven o'clock news at channel 3, I didn't go into work until around three o'clock. Normally I would grab the mail before heading in, and this one day in August of 1981, I heard the mail drop through the slot in my front door. I remember looking at the pile of mail and pulling out the latest *New York* magazine. There on the cover staring back at me was the cast of *LIVE AT FIVE*, the 5:00 P.M. newscast of the flagship station of NBC. There were anchors Sue Simmons and Jack Cafferty along with famed gossip columnist Liz Smith. Also featured were reviewer Katie Kelly and resident feature reporter Chauncey Howell. To complete the team was television weather legend Dr. Frank Field. The headline was "THE HOTTEST SHOW ON TV." Wow. I will never be part of anything that big, I thought while looking at it.

Back in 1981 there was no *E! News. Entertainment Tonight* had just started. There had been nothing like *Live at Five* on TV. It had the traditional elements of a broadcast, but a few key differences. As I studied the cover of the magazine, I noticed that no one on it resembled the Doug Adairs of the world. None of these people fit into the stereotypical newscaster mold; they looked like real people. Sue was brazen, whip smart, *and black*. And Katie Kelly had massive hair, nerdy glasses, and wore a bowtie!

They had personalities and they let them show. I put the magazine down and decided it was time to just head into work and do my job. But the more I thought about it, who knows—maybe I could go further than I thought I could. Maybe I could be part of something much bigger.

ALTRUISM #7

Madness without a Reason
Is Straight-Up Insanity

EVERY MORNING as the clock strikes 7:00 A.M., *The Today Show* starts on NBC. You hear the *dah-DAH-dah!* . . . and then a voice-over, maybe Savannah, narrating any breaking news. She'll go on to detail the major stories she'll be covering that morning, from Iran, fires and floods, to developments in the White House. The camera will open on a shot of Hoda and Savannah— the picture of poise, control, and confidence—all smiles, ready to deliver you the hard-hitting news. While what you see unfolding during the broadcast may appear calm and professional, I guarantee you that for every smiling broadcaster there are at least six people cursing in the background. I think this is likely true of many industries where calm and precision are required.

I once did a piece on *Today* where I swapped jobs with the famous French chef Daniel Boulud. His restaurant, Daniel, has two Michelin stars and is the picture of elegance. Think soft lighting, crisp linens, and gleaming silver. Bright spots of color grace each table in the form of fresh flowers. Even the air tastes good at Daniel. This is one seriously classy joint I'm talking about here. Jackets are required for gentlemen, which is the kind of old-school thing that I just get all warm and fuzzy about.

I have known Daniel for over thirty years. During my time at WNBC I was assigned to interview him for a piece about rising new chefs, when he was just starting out. He must have felt I was a trustworthy guy, because he handed over his newborn baby, Alix, for me to hold while he was showing me around the restaurant. We kept in touch and even developed a friendship over the years. A top-chef pal is another hugely positive side effect of my job. The producers wanted Daniel to do the weather during *The Today Show* and I would be "helping out" in his kitchen. Me, Albert Lincoln Roker Jr., ruler of my backyard barbecue, would get to "cook" in the kitchen of a Michelin-starred restaurant! But wait! What was I thinking? It occurred to me that if people actually preferred their weather from a worldly, erudite, good-looking Frenchman with a thick accent I would have a problem.

The night before, I could barely concentrate on what was going on at home during dinner; all I could do was imagine myself donned in kitchen whites, preparing Daniel's famous paupiette of sea bass or pot-au-feu royale. I'd finally be able to test-drive the basic knife skills I'd honed over the years. I'd produce a gorgeous pile of identically cut sticks of carrots and the staff would be like, "Mon Dieu! Monsieur Roker, your bâtonnet! C'est parfait! You really know your way around la cuisine!" I'd be like, "Oh, you guys, thanks! I'm just really so glad I could be helpful." The reality of what happened was quite different.

Behind the swinging door of one of New York City's most sophisticated restaurants you will find a war zone. Or the kitchen equivalent of one. I stepped into the kitchen to find shouting, cursing, and dangerously hot objects being moved around at breakneck speeds. The temperature of the kitchen was approximately one thousand degrees! I didn't know how to begin to insert myself into this fray. I couldn't imagine a single thing I could do that would be at all helpful. I was considering sneaking out of the kitchen, totally abandoning my film crew, flying out the back door, and hailing a cab before anyone in the kitchen noticed I was there.

That's when I heard: "Hey, you."

With much apprehension, I responded: "Me?"

One of the line chefs pointed to an entrée that looked as if the yuzu-wasabi-marinated yellowfin tuna had been garnished by the hands of God. "Yeah, you. See that F#&king entrée right there? If you don't get that out now I'm going to stab you in the F#&king eye with a boning knife."

I stood there frozen. As still as glass. Message received!

The rest of the evening I hustled in a blur of sweat and fear as I tried to stay the hell out of everyone's way. The night went by in a haze of onion chopping. When it was discovered I was competent enough not to sever a finger, they let me help the expeditor garnish plates.

It seemed that a night at Daniel was deemed a success if I didn't leave in a body bag with a meat cleaver sticking out of my chest. To be clear, I was not actually stabbed in the eye by anyone working for Daniel Boulud. Nor was I upset or offended in any way—just temporarily terrified. And it was not Daniel himself threatening me. It was his executive chef who was doing his job . . . and obviously he was some sort of manic perfectionist. (I get it! They have Michelin stars to maintain!)

I understood this sort of operation. From my experience in newsrooms this was a finely tuned team; they had their methodologies mastered. To toss some inexperienced weatherperson into that mix was a big no-no. They worked with precision, and that's why they were the best. He probably wasn't a bad guy, but there was no time for pleasantries such as "Excuse me, dear Al, would you mind terribly moving this entrée before it gets a wee bit cold?" He just really needed to get me the F#&k out of the way so he could do his job right.

Your beautifully plated filet mignon is the result of a crazy amount of behind-the-scenes activity—and it's not necessarily pretty. The kitchen staff have their own culture and are working an incredibly high-pressured job at a pace that moves faster than your typical October hurricane. It was a marvel to witness.

I AM NOT CONDONING any kind of abuse at work. Nor do I operate in that manner. But I am well familiar with the overall vibe of the control room—and it is lunacy. The language tossed around back there is not for tender ears. When we show the control room on *The Today Show* but without audio, it's for a reason.*

In Syracuse, my dear mentor Andy Brigham was known for this gem:

"No matter how hard you try, you can't chrome-plate shit."

Yet, people try. Oh, they try! In Cleveland, an assistant news director named Cliff decided he didn't like my glasses. You know who else didn't like my glasses? *Me!* I have worn glasses every day since first grade at PS 272. I had been complaining to my teacher Mrs. Hamburger (the principal was named Grimace—*buh-dum-tsssss!*) that I couldn't see the blackboard. My mother dragged me off to the optometrist where I received my very first pair of black-framed glasses with Coke-bottle lenses. And I've worn glasses every single day of my life since.

Cliff had a plan. "So, Roker, when the light hits your glasses it reflects off them and it's very distracting." I didn't like the way this was going. If they made me take them off I wouldn't be able to see a thing. I'd be wandering around the set unable to see the crew, green screen, maps,

---

*Rather than show an actual shot from the control room on live television the other day, we chose to show the iconic painting *Dogs Playing Poker* by Cassius Marcellus Coolridge instead. We felt it adequately captured its essence. We also do our best to avoid fines from the FCC whenever we can at *Today*.

cameras, lights, and nine million cables it takes to create a newscast. What could possibly go wrong on live television in this scenario?

"Well, the thing is, I need my glasses to see."

The guy laughed. "Oh, we're not going to make you get rid of your glasses!" Continuing: "No! We're going to get you contacts, and because we like *the look* of your glasses we're going to pop the lenses out! No glare! Problem solved!" This sounded like one of the dumbest ideas ever!

"So, I'll be wearing contact lenses but then also a pair of empty frames?" Cliff nodded. No doubt about it—this guy was trying to chrome-plate a total shit idea.

In the 1970s there were no such things as soft, disposable contact lenses. Contacts were hard—they were made out of *glass*. It wasn't at all unusual to be in a public place, say the shopping mall or a movie theater, and hear a person shout out: "Don't move, anyone! I've lost a contact!" Everyone, regardless of age or social status, would participate in a frantic search. Contacts were expensive! It must be found! A collective cheer would be heard when that slippery little bastard was located, or there'd be a collective groan when everyone heard the distinctive sound that was a contact lens being crushed by a foot.

The day we were rolling out my non-glasses finally arrived. As I was getting ready to go on, I noticed my eyes didn't feel right. It almost felt like there were glass orbs floating around in my eyeballs . . . oh wait! There were! I started blinking uncontrollably and I couldn't stop. I get the countdown, and I'm blinking like a madman. It's like my eyeballs were rejecting this totally shit idea.

"Here's Al Roker with the weather!" I'm on. I'm doing my forecast and I'm blinking. "Rain is expected." Blinking. "But things will clear up!" Blinking. And to make matters worse I know I look ridiculous, because I'm wearing glasses with no freakin' glass in them!! I'm wearing frames with no F#&king lenses.

After my broadcast the switchboard lights right up. The calls come rolling in: "Why is Al Roker trying to signal the audience in Morse code? What's wrong with his eyes?" and "What is wrong with Al? Why is he wearing glasses without glass? Has he lost his mind?" So, I've got to point something out here. No one cared enough that a black man was doing the weather to make a phone call—but it's the madly blinking weather guy in the empty frames that sets people off? The phones were ringing like crazy.

This turd in the punchbowl of an idea, as I suspected, did not take to chrome plating. Thankfully the assistant news director agreed. I got my real glasses back.

But I mean, c'mon. Have you ever managed to turn something truly awful into something glorious and shiny? You can't! Shit is to be avoided at all costs. Don't step in it!

John Lynch, a veteran stage manager I would encounter later in my career during my WNBC days, distilled his disdain for some of the folks in the newsroom with a little bon mot that I never forgot. The newscast was moving along fine; one of the reporters was doing a piece on getting last-minute reservations to restaurants on Valentine's Day. She was speaking to a maître d' at a popular local restaurant: "So, if you haven't made Valentine's plans and you're really in the doghouse, is there anything you can try to do to get a reservation?" The maître d' replied, "Actually, yes!" and just as he proceeded to spill the secret of getting an "impossible" last-minute dinner reservation (and as we all know, potentially saving a relationship) the audio operator in the control room turned on the music that signaled the piece was over. No one heard a damn thing the guy said.

Afterwards, I heard John, frustrated and speaking to no one in particular . . . "These guys couldn't ad-lib a fart after a six-course Hungarian dinner."*

FROM WARNINGS ABOUT chrome-plating poop to the hazards of six-course Hungarian dinners, each workplace has its own special quirks and oddities that must be sorted through. As a guy who has been sworn at in a professional

---

*Hungarian dishes are known to contain sausage, paprika, and *cabbage*. Six courses. Do the math.

kitchen and been made to wear lens-free eyeglasses on live television, I understand how alarming this can be. However, once you get past the surface of yelling, cursing, or whatever freakiness you happen to encounter, there's often a worthwhile endeavor happening (if there isn't, run for the hills) and a reason for all the madness. To produce something great there's usually a lot of sweat, blood, and tears involved. To grow and get to the next level of your career and in life you must be prepared to encounter scenarios you didn't expect—that you don't feel adequately prepared for. And once you finally learn to roll with the punches, you'll see that while things are not always what they seem, it's usually worth all the trouble in the end.

ALTRUISM #8

Get Your Piece
of the Pie

WNBC (the NBC-owned and -operated station in New York City) was missing a weekend weatherperson. For a year and a half after Cliff Morrison's departure, the weekend weather was done by a rotating cast of characters. I had nine months to go on my contract in Cleveland, also owned by NBC; I was content, but it was still a goal to get back to New York City. My boss, Kris Ostrowski, called me into her office one day. "Al, have you got a minute? I want to talk to you about something." Hmm, I was suspicious. I couldn't think of anything I had done that would get me into hot water. "Oh, Al, great. I'm glad you can talk. Can you close the door?" Close the door? Oh no!

I sat down across from Kris, who had a slightly mischievous smile on her face. "Al, I think you should apply for that job in New York." This wasn't what I expected to hear. Was Kris trying to get rid of me? I knew about the position in New York—word spreads amongst weather forecasters—but I hadn't seriously considered it for one important reason: it was part time. Weather on weekends only. "I appreciate the idea, Kris, but here I get to do the weather every day." Kris sighed. "Al, it's an opportunity to go back to New York. You should go for it. Call your agent." When I talked to Alfred about the opportunity—adding that my current boss was telling me to go—he said,

"No one ever does that, kid. You're working with someone of high principle there." With Kris's blessing, I flew out for an interview and was offered the job. But there was a small catch: I couldn't leave until they filled my position.

It took a few months to find my replacement, and during that time I had become full of doubts about leaving. The job in New York paid less because it was part time, and if there's one thing I knew about New York it's that the cost of living is *bananas*. Would I be able to manage? Would I have to live in one of those old-timey apartments that has a bathtub in the middle of the kitchen? Or I could live with my parents? Nothing says you're succeeding at life like living with your parents when you're nearly thirty! To make matters more complicated, I was going through a divorce and was really leaning on my friends for support. Things had come full circle for me in Cleveland, and I wasn't sure I wanted to go. I was like the kid who gets dropped off at camp screaming and kicking—*No, I don't want to be here! It's unfamiliar! Who are these people?*

The network offered to double my salary if I stayed to help drive the team to the number one slot. So, double the money to live in a city I've come to love, where I have terrific friends and colleagues? Or move to New York, where my entire salary would barely cover the rent on a closet? Going "home" was starting to lose its appeal.

I called Alfred. "Al, I'm thinking of staying in Cleveland. I don't want to go to New York." I could practically hear Alfred's eyes popping out of his head. "Al, I'm not calling them. Think about this for another day." I hung up the phone, and I didn't feel any better. My gut was telling me the city would be exciting—that even though I was comfortable, I should run off to the big city and give it a go! But my heavy heart was saying, Stick around, you've got it good here. You're going to leave a full-time job for part-time work? As soon as I put the phone down it rang again. "Al, it's Kris. I heard you're not thinking of going to New York. As your boss—well, that's terrific for me. I'd love to keep you. But as a friend, I've got to tell you you're about to make the worst mistake of your life. It's time for you to go." I wasn't 100 percent sure it was the right thing to do, but it was worth a shot. At the very least, my mom could finally watch me on TV in the comfort of her own home, down one channel slot from channel 5 to 4!

I MOVED BACK to New York City in 1984, and I was determined for it to be a fresh start.

I wanted to mark the occasion that I had landed back in the city, so I took myself to the stationery department at Barneys New York, an exclusive department store in Manhattan that has just shuttered its doors in New York City and all across the country. I spotted a Filofax made of a rich brown leather with trimming that added to its air of sophistication. It was the sort of leather that would likely grow darker and softer with age. The calendar pages were the perfect size for my large scripted handwriting, and the address book section had been perfectly curated. The lined paper for notes seemed to be extra bright, and the makers of this masterpiece had included just the right amount. I imagined the pages of the Filofax would soon fill up with important contacts and appointments, big ideas, and restaurant recommendations for lunch dates. (Long before anyone had ever heard of an iPhone or Apple watch, the Filofax was the status symbol that said *I'm someone and I'm super busy*.)

After touching, gently inspecting (and maybe even smelling), the Filofax, I asked a salesperson the price. $150! I winced for a second. It was more money than I had spent on...like, anything! Well, I did have a "champagne"-colored Volkswagen Rabbit convertible. Sorry, it was the eighties! This Filofax was such a thing of beauty that I knew I couldn't leave it behind. I bought the Filofax for nearly $150 (that's over 370 bucks in 2020 dollars for a phone book!). It represented promise—a sign that my career and life were looking up, and they were. Although, I had to remind myself, I was currently living in a hotel (albeit a nice one).

I had a lovely diary for writing down all of my appointments, but I didn't technically have a place to live. Finding an apartment in New York City is about as much fun as dental surgery without Novocain. And who am I to judge?

First there's the matter of traipsing all over the city to actually look at the apartments. Then once you've weeded out the ones that resemble jail cells or have walls so thin it sounds like you're living in a night club, there's the matter of being first in line to get it. In Manhattan one must wage battle with others for an overpriced box. When I was in college up in Syracuse, I could only imagine that I'd live in Manhattan someday. The act of moving from the outer boroughs to the island of Manhattan was for movers and shakers, the ambitious—those who finally got *a piece of the pie* à la George Jefferson.

Finding a place is a drama of epic proportions that I thankfully did not have to embark on this time around. I was blessed with a "relocation package." NBC put me up temporarily in their corporate lodgings. NBC didn't mess around either. For eight glorious weeks I got to live at the St. Regis, one of the finest hotels in all of New York City. To a guy who grew up in a three-bedroom, one-bath house in Queens with his parents and five siblings (need to use the bathroom? Take a number and good luck to you!), to say I was *movin' on up* was an understatement. The hotel is the definition of old-school beauty. They literally invented the Bloody Mary.* Before booking an ill-fated passage

---

*The folks at the St. Regis originally called it the Red Snapper, lest anyone be offended that a brunch cocktail (often associated with hangovers) share a name with the Blessed Mother.

on the *Titanic,* John Jacob Astor IV founded the St. Regis Hotel because he needed "a place to work and socialize amongst the city's elite." Determined it be a technologically advanced hotel, Astor insisted that each room have its very own telephone. It's like the St. Regis is the ancient ancestor of co-working spaces. I was temporarily living in the lap of luxury.

When my first day of the new job arrived I walked through the lobby of the St. Regis, with equal parts nervousness and excitement, and onto Fifty-Fifth Street, where the rush-hour-traffic noise of eager taxis and marching bands of people moving at top speed in their trench coats and sneakers hit me full blast. I had grown accustomed to tranquil midwestern Cleveland, getting into my car on my quiet suburban street, and peacefully driving downtown to work. Nope, not in New York. While I was marveling over this change in circumstance, I was jolted back to attention by a man shouting at me on the street. "Hey, why you just standing there? Get outta the way, buddy!" I snapped to attention and started moving with the fray.

I turned south onto Fifth Avenue, quickening my pace to keep up. It felt good to be part of this busy group of people—all of us with somewhere important to be. We were the crème of the crop professionals. And I was excited to learn from the greats. At the corner of Fiftieth Street I stopped in front of St. Patrick's Cathedral and crossed over to Rockefeller Center. I had fond memories of taking family trips to Rockefeller Center with my parents to see the Christmas tree lighting during the holidays. To my young eyes, it was always a classic experience, like something out of the movies, with the skaters gliding around beneath the ever-watchful eyes of the gold Prometheus statue. When I entered 30 Rock as Big Al, and saw the art deco lobby and the field of gleaming black marble floors, I stopped and took a breath. *Wow. This is where I work? I feel like I've made it to the great land of Oz.*

Once I got settled, the producers told me the plan was for me to spend my first two weeks shadowing the great Frank Field, a living legend in the world of broadcast news. Frank did the weather Monday through Friday at WNBC. He was so beloved throughout the city that many people in New York thought of him as an uncle or old family friend. He became a frequent guest on *The Tonight Show Starring Johnny Carson.* Should Frank have predicted sunny skies only to be surprised by an afternoon rain shower, Johnny would rip him a new one on national television. Frank was a mild-mannered, bespectacled gentleman with such a dry sense of humor. He would just laugh at Johnny's dig—he never took himself too seriously. Let's set the record straight: weatherfolks do get the weather wrong.

And if you ever nearly choked to death but lived to tell about it, chances are you have Frank Field to thank for that. Field was an early pioneer of the Heimlich maneuver. Before instructional posters about how to perform the

Heimlich were commonly plastered on the walls of restaurants, approximately five thousand Americans died from "café coronary syndrome" every year. At the urging of Dr. Heimlich himself, Field demonstrated the life-saving maneuver on live television. In an extraordinary twist of fate, Field would nearly succumb to café coronary syndrome himself. In 1985, a year after he left WNBC for the greener pastures of WCBS-TV, Frank was dining at a tavern on Eleventh Avenue with Warner Wolf, WCBS's sports guy. Suddenly, Field found himself choking on a chunk of roast beef. Luckily, Wolf had learned from Field's demonstration. He jumped up and executed the Heimlich and the roast beef popped right out. Wolf saved Field from death as well as the embarrassment of dying from the very cause he was determined to save people from. But that ironic near-death experience was still a year away when I first met Frank Field.

The original plan was that I'd follow Frank around for two weeks and do my first forecast on a Saturday. I'd get the lay of the land, learn about any differences between the way we did things back in Cleveland and at WNBC. "C'mon, Roker. Let's go down to the weather service. It's on the mezzanine," Frank said after a few hours on the first day, while I sat at my desk twirling my pen in mini carousels awaiting his summons. Frank and I took the elevator down from the sixth floor and retrieved a satellite image off a telefax. (A fax machine is like a printer merged with a phone line. Ask your parents.) *This is it?* I thought to myself. I was shocked by this primitive process. WNBC was living in the Dark Ages—my local station in Cleveland had better technology than this. As we were making our way back to the studio, I asked Frank: "Where's the weather computer? Where do we get the graphics?" Frank just walked over to an easel that was placed on the set, slapped the picture on it, and said, "Right there. There's your graphic." By the time he did the forecast, that image would be six hours old. Was this the best they could do here? I took a deep breath and reminded myself that I was in the biggest market now—who cares if I'm pointing to a picture of a rain cloud rather than real footage?

A few days into my new job Frank said, "So, how are you feeling about this, Al?" Technology worries aside, I was adjusting to the changes. It wasn't like my new gig at WNBC required me to do a back flip at the end of every forecast. The territory was familiar enough. I took a quick self-assessment. "You know what, Frank? I'm feeling pretty good about this."

Field's eyes lit up. "Fantastic. It's settled. You'll do the forecast tomorrow. I'm taking the day off!"

And with that announcement Frank grabbed his briefcase, tossed his overcoat over one shoulder, and walked out the door.

I had just started on Monday and wasn't supposed to be on the air for nearly another week and a half! That confidence I'd felt just a few minutes ago quickly bolted from my body out the door. Was I really ready for this? Apparently Frank thought so. I took another deep breath—who am I to argue with a life-saving weather forecaster? I went home that night and didn't get much sleep, imagining my run-ins with the paper clouds for all of New York to see. I hoped my mom wouldn't watch.

The next day as I walked into the newsroom Bret Marcus, who produced the 6:00 P.M. broadcast, saw me and called out, "Hey, uhh . . . Roker, right? Where's Frank?"

I tried to hide my alarm. I assumed Frank would have cleared it with the producers that I was taking his place! "Ummm, home?"

Bret looked like he didn't know what I was talking about, mildly alarmed, as if he wanted to ask, *What are you saying, dimwit?*

"Oh. It's okay. I'm filling in for him," I added. "He told me to come."

The expression on Bret's face no longer suggested light concern. He looked at me like I had just stomped on the paws of his brand-new puppy. On purpose. "Get the F#&k outta here. This is the first I've heard of this!"

Okay, so not the reaction I was hoping for, but I told myself that everything would be fine. Nothing to worry about here! Just then the producer of *Live at Five*, Sue Levine. heard the tail end of the conversation and joined in with a much more reassuring "Who the F#&k are you?"

I wanted to mash myself up into a small ball and roll on out of there. *Who was I?* Suddenly I didn't know. Sue Levine was known for being no-nonsense, a take-charge New Yorker who didn't suffer fools or fill-in weatherpeople gladly. This woman didn't mess around. And now I had both these producers looking at me like they were wondering if I had, in fact, tied Field up and locked him in a closet. I needed to explain what was going on, quick. "I know I'm not supposed to start until next weekend, but Frank told me to fill in for him. I thought he'd tell everyone?" The explanation just seemed to encourage more fury. "Are you serious? Get the F#&k outta here!" With Sue's emphasis on the "outta here" I was confused about whether she meant that I should indeed exit. I sort of wobbled in place.

"Well, I can tell you no one told me!" Bret added. "Where the F#&k is Frank for Christ's sake?" I was beginning to sense the f-bomb was very popular here. Bret was so exasperated that his face had turned beet red. "Wait a minute. Does Bob Davis know?" Bret tossed his hands in the air to indicate that this was serious! Now we're getting the news director involved! I wanted to run out of there. The air in the room was heavy with tension, more akin to what I'd expect in the situation room at the White House. Everyone started scrambling for Bob's whereabouts. Bret didn't know what to do about the show, now that Frank had flatlined the production by inviting this newbie that no one knew anything about to replace him. "And what's your name again?" he'd ask every few minutes, stroking his beard. I'd come to learn that Bret's nickname was "Hamlet" because of his infamous indecision. "To be or not to be"— that was always Bret's question. Before he was married, everybody joked that he was single because women would ask him "Your place or mine?" Bret wouldn't be able to decide. Bret didn't know what to do, until finally the news director, Bob, arrived. He walked up to me calmly and said, "Listen. From now on, you got to let me know about these kinds of changes, okay? I've got to know what's going on, you understand?" I shrugged my shoulders. Sure, I understood. I wanted to say maybe some of the powers that be could go ahead and mention that to FRANK!

NEW OPPORTUNITIES, whether a new job, school, or moving to a new town, can be exciting, but they're also overwhelming. There's so much to get used to. You're just getting your bearings, meeting new faces, and figuring out important stuff like "Where exactly do people get the good donuts around here?" And "For God's sake, where is the men's room on this floor?" That takes time.

Change of any sort is unsettling. Well, it can be for me. And the first time you encounter an obstacle (a group of news producers who are cursing you out) it's really easy to think you've made a huge mistake. The *what-the-hell-was-I-thinking* feeling is the worst, but chances are it will lead to the best opportunity of your life. I wonder if Deborah thought that after our first date. Too bad, I'm her lucky husband today! (Cheese!)

I was standing on set, about to go on WNBC for the first time, and flashing through my mind was ... What am I doing here when I could be back in Cleveland where we had an actual computer to forecast the weather instead of this stupid easel? What is this, kindergarten art class?

I was plotting how I could get my old job back when one of the producers yelled that I should take my place on set, *Live at Five* was starting. I took a breath, got myself focused, and listened to the countdown: three, two, one ... Legendary anchor Sue Simmons said, "Joining us now is the newest member of News 4, Al Roker, in for Dr. Frank Field. Al, welcome." "Thanks, Sue," came out of my mouth, and I've been doing the weather in New York ever since. Everything just felt right. Swearing, concerns about doing the weather only part time, that ridiculous easel, leaving my friends behind—none of it mattered. I was telling the fine citizens of New York City, my hometown, what to expect from the weather today. My parents were probably watching me at this very moment! I kept moving through the forecast, and it felt great. I really did have my own piece of the pie! It didn't matter that it wasn't perfect ... *it was mine.* I had a long road ahead of me (how can I make them buy a computer!?), but I had gotten a sense of what the reward would be, and I wanted more. I was doing what I wanted to do, where I wanted to do it, and that was amazing! Who does that?! I learned from out the gate moving to WNBC, and during those first three days at work, when you're in the midst of change, just stay the course. People always ask how I've kept my job for so long, or how I do so many jobs! One of the secrets is to be able to just change course. Move in the direction the wind takes you (I can do weather puns all day). When all of that newness wears off (and it will), you'll most likely discover you're happy to be right where you are.

ALTRUISM #9

Crying in Your
Oatmeal-Soy-Almond Latte
Never Helps Anything

I WAS THE WEEKEND WEATHERPERSON who did the 6 and 11:00 P.M. news on Saturdays and Sundays, and to get their money's worth out of me, I did fluffy feature pieces Wednesday through Friday. I was especially excited when I was asked to do my first piece outside of the studio. Taking things to the street, if you will, was going to be a new experience. It was a fun story about the different manhole covers that adorn our city streets. They really are works of art, and they were created by different foundries. For the opening of my piece I decided to add a flare of drama by lying down on the street with my head directly next to a manhole cover. (Are you grossed out by my head on a NYC street? Hey, I like to get really involved.) I used my most serious voice to intone: "Manhole covers. Works of art or portal to another dimension? You decide!"

About a week later, it was time for my first live shot. I was doing the weather in Central Park because it was unusually warm for December. We were all ready to go. I heard the associate director in my ear via my earpiece, which was connected to the control room at 30 Rock, say, "Thirty seconds," then suddenly, seemingly out of nowhere, the cameraman, a grizzled photographer named Joey Gaffa, moved from behind the camera, locked eyes with me, and said sternly, "For the next two minutes, I am

NBC and I own you." *Own me?* Then he moved back behind the camera.

Suddenly, I heard News 4 anchorman Chuck Scarborough say, "Now here's Al Roker with the latest on this unusually warm December day, live from Central Park . . . Al?" The voice from the control room said, "Cue" in my ear. *Wait! What?* I didn't know if I was ready. The psycho behind the camera had just given me a death threat. Somehow my mouth kept moving and I got through my piece, but during my whole forecast I wondered why such a dramatic assertion of power needed to be announced. Was he serious? Was he going to beat me up after work? After we got an all-clear from the control room, he poked his head from behind the camera and smiled. "Nice job, kid!"

"Uh, thanks," I said, happy to be alive. Turns out, Joey was kidding. Just a little hazing of the new guy. I discovered he was one of the nicest guys around.

The crew started packing up, so I bent down to pick up a tripod.

Coming from Cleveland, everybody pitched in to break down, pack up, and head home. Even though it was a union shop, we all helped each other out. And that's when my help was rewarded with "Just what the F#&k do you think you're doing with that tripod, buddy?" from one of the guys on the crew.

I froze. "Uhhh, putting it back down?" I dropped the tripod like it was dripping toxic waste.

"F#&kin'-A, you are!!"

Obviously, we are not in Cleveland anymore, Toto.

I was accustomed to helping the crew in Cleveland, and in Syracuse we literally did everything ourselves. It wasn't like the film *Groundhog Day* where Phil Connors just showed up at an appointed time, was handed a microphone, and started talking when someone pointed at him. Our method of producing a story in Syracuse was like this: My camera person, usually a crackerjack named Marge, and I got into our crew car. It was anything from a Ford Bronco to a Ford Pinto because the station had a trade deal with a local Ford dealership. We were assigned tour stops by our producer or assignment editor. We'd end up somewhere like in front of a giant mural of the governor made of popsicles surrounded by Girl Scouts. Marge would run the camera, capturing the cuteness while I spoke. We would pack up our gear and hit the next spot. This time, I would run camera and Marge would be the reporter. It was two for the price of one!

We shot all the footage on actual film—video had yet to arrive. It's easy nowadays to forget that film must be developed, because today teenagers are earning an income equal to the GDP of a mid-sized European country by creating YouTube videos of themselves putting on makeup. But the pre-Tubers like us had to think long and hard about what we wanted to shoot before pressing the button on any camera. Is a vacation picture of my beautifully manicured foot worthy of a photo album? In the day of film, no self-respecting person would have wasted a shot on cappuccino art, that's for sure.

After taking turns shooting our pieces, we'd have to dash over to the developer, a quirky man named Cosmo,* who would develop our film, leaving it to be picked up by each station's chief photographer, who would deliver it to the station within a couple of hours. In our case, it was a guy named John Ellis who would take the day's output of news film and divvy it up to be left on our respective desks. Then we would take it to an available film-editing bay and physically edit our own news story, cutting and splicing after banging out a script on a battered typewriter. It was clunky and, by today's standards, crude. But it was fun. You were really responsible for every facet of your story and the end result.

This sounds so old-fashioned today that it probably gives the impression I'm writing this from the confines of an easy chair. You're probably envisioning me wearing a bathrobe and draped in an afghan to ward off the chill, while drinking Ensure and waiting for someone to bring me my walker. But that experience gave me and every other TV journalist an advantage. We knew how to

---

*No one was more surprised than I was when the *Seinfeld* character Kramer's first name turned out to be Cosmo. I mean, really, what are the odds?

collaborate and put a piece together properly. We understood how each aspect of the process worked. But during
my early days in New York, it was becoming clear that my
"help" wasn't needed—I just needed to do my job and get
the hell out of everyone's way.

MEANWHILE, BACK INSIDE the studio the awkwardness about filling in for Frank continued, as it would for
the next six months of my life. Frank would suddenly
announce: "Roker! You're filling in," and the pattern of
annoyance/disbelief/f-bombs/fine-I-guess-Roker-is-
doing-the-weather was set in motion once again. I'd come
home to my fancy hotel and ponder how to deal with this.
I could handle this situation two ways. (1) I could let myself
be overcome by dread every time I heard "Roker! I need
you to fill in for me tomorrow, thanks a lot!" knowing the
producers would be irritated once again—*with me.* Or (2)
I could embrace this strange scenario knowing that I was
getting on-air time, doing a job I loved, and every extra
broadcast made me better at my craft. So what if I got
the stink eye. *Sticks and stones, people!* Their reaction, and
Frank's lack of communication, was something I couldn't
change. The only way to win this one was to become good
at doing the weather. Eventually, just maybe, someday I'd
walk into the newsroom unexpected and hear "Nice to see

you, Al. Are you doing the weather today? Terrific!" Rather than "Where the freak is Frank?" One could dream.

MY REGULAR BROADCASTS, plus all the ones I ended up covering for Frank, kept me working hard. Weekends did not exist; everything was about work. My Filofax was filling up, but not quite how I had hoped. The pages were filled with work, work, and more work. I'd sit down every Sunday night and study the times I'd have to be at the station, which were essentially daily and at all hours. There were times I wanted to be doing something else—something fun like a movie, a walk, a dinner out with friends—but before the pity party commenced I'd think about my dad. My dad's business through all of my childhood was bus driving. If there was ever an opportunity to work more and earn more, he took it. In February of 1967, more than a foot of snow landed in New York City in a twelve-hour period. If the excessive snow wasn't enough to keep you inside that day, the mind-numbing cold might have. That day had a high of just sixteen degrees, but wind gusts made it feel like somewhere in the neighborhood of negative five to fifteen. My father gathered me and my siblings in the kitchen early that morning. He explained that he had snow bus patrol and he'd be out in the thick of it, delivering supplies and making sure the stops were cleared out. "I'm probably not going to see you guys for nearly a week," he said. "I'll be sleeping at the depot. You all listen to your mom, okay? This is a good opportunity to make some extra money." We all understood the importance of Dad's work. Although we were still young when he bought the house in Queens, I think we all understood it was the long extra hours that made it a reality.

My dad taught me about how hard work made things possible. Who cared if I couldn't spend a balmy afternoon waltzing through Central Park. I was staying in the St. Regis sleeping on sheets with a never-ending thread count! When I first got to NBC and hadn't had a day off in ages, I used to eat lunch in the NBC commissary. I'd go up there to take a quick break and enjoy what I believed to be the city's finest grilled cheese and bacon sandwich. While grilled cheese sandwiches are sadly no longer part of my lunch repertoire, the NBC commissary's grilled cheese was a thing of beauty. It's like their grilled cheese was aspirational—it was the grilled cheese all other sandwiches tried but failed to be. It boasted the perfect combo of cheese, buttered white bread, and bacon—toasted to perfection on a grill that had been serving up all manner of fried items for decades. It's possible NBC had the most well-seasoned grill in all of Manhattan.

The walls of the NBC commissary were painted baby-crap yellow. The thick cinder-block walls were reminiscent of a jail cell (no windows!) and the unnatural florescent lighting made everyone in the place look slightly ill. The smell of stale cigarette smoke was baked into the cracked, laminated tables. And I loved all of it. Sitting at a scuffed-up table drinking a cup of bitter, slightly odd-smelling coffee, I could witness the history of NBC unfolding right before my eyes. It wasn't unusual to see Tom Brokaw from the nightly news come in to grab lunch. John Lovitz, Billy Crystal, and Dana Carvey might be huddled together working on a script, throwing back pools of coffee. The commissary was like the great equalizer: we all need to eat—everyone is welcome here. It was like NBC's community center. You never knew who you were going to see—the cast of *Saturday Night Live*, a famous news anchor, or your favorite security guard. The grilled cheeses were so good that sometimes I'd go back for another (I was prone to indulging in seconds in those days). I'd eat my sandwich sitting there looking at all of the people. In that room news was put together, comedy skits were written, and ideas were flowing. I marveled that I was part of it. It was a reminder that if I worked hard, stayed focused, and didn't waste my time having a big *oh, woe is me party* I could make a difference here. The cafeteria showed that all of our contributions mattered—even the guy's who made the world's greatest grilled cheese.

IT IS SO EASY in the early years of your career, business, or any new venture you're taking on to think things are never going to change. You'll never take a proper vacation, never earn enough money, you'll always be grinding away like a peasant as you grapple with the totem pole. There was a period in my early years at WNBC when I worked eight weeks straight with only two days off. Dr. Field had gotten into a contract dispute and left channel 4 for what he thought were the greener pastures of WCBS, and so I had to fill in. It was exhausting and difficult, but I was focused on reaching my goals, not achieving the ideal work–life balance. I was not tempted to quit to find a less grueling position. I wanted to see where this job could take me.

I know it's hard to be at the bottom of the totem pole, but there's no need to cry in your oatmeal-soy-almond-milk latte (insert latte of choice here). Everything feels monumental when you're down there! Every mistake feels life defining! Decades have passed (yes, decades plural, young people) since I was a full-fledged newbie, and I can tell you that your life and career will not always look like they do today. Those worries about balance and personal time fall away as you forge ahead. So many good things come of sticking it out and putting roots down at work and in your passion. It's worth it in the end. And lastly, as a very wise man I once met in passing said, "Never underestimate just knowing where the bathrooms are."

ALTRUISM #10

Get Up an Hour Before
You Need To

I REALIZE I DID NOT INVENT the concept of time, but as someone who has woken up at 3:45 A.M. for nearly forty years, I do consider myself an authority on the matter. Tim Cook, Oprah, Michelle Obama, and US Navy SEALs also get up absurdly early, so apparently I'm in good company. Mark Wahlberg gets up at 2:30 A.M. That guy is definitely taking it too far. Why on earth would anyone need to work out at 2:30 A.M.?

I love waking up early because most of the country is still asleep and you've already done a spin class. Bravo! The transition to waking up before the official crack of dawn wasn't hard for me; I've always been an early riser. When I was a kid, my dad woke up early for his shifts at the bus depot. I'd get up and eat breakfast with him. After eating I would watch him shine his shoes and get ready to head off to work. As the oldest of six it quickly became clear that this was the best way I could get alone time with my dad. I'd go back upstairs after he left, pretend I was just waking up, and get ready to reemerge in the kitchen just in time for a second breakfast with my siblings.* WIN-Win!

Getting up early has been hard-wired into my life, but once—just once—I overslept, and the ramifications were

---

*The bonus breakfast was obviously also a huge draw to getting up early.

incredible. For six years I was also doing a show called *Wake Up with Al* at 5:00 A.M. on the Weather Channel. The show was shot across the street from *The Today Show* on the sixth floor of our iconic NBC headquarters, 30 Rockefeller Plaza. After my 5:00 A.M. gig wrapped up, I'd just dash across the street to get ready for *Today*. But on August 6, 2013, I overslept. I did not wake up. Nothing out of the ordinary preceded this—I hadn't been traveling internationally, nor was I was up all night smoking cigars and playing poker with the guys. When the alarm went off at 3:45, I apparently ignored it and remained in the comfort of my bed for several more hours. When I finally woke up at 6:00 A.M., I noticed the time and thought, Holy s$*t!

I flew out of bed and lunged for my cell phone. There were about five thousand messages from my producers, who were concerned about my well-being. It was feared I had been kidnapped, dropped dead of a heart attack—or maybe just woke up and decided, I'm done with all of this! I shall devote today to tai chi and learning the traditional art of sand mandalas! Seeing as I hadn't overslept in thirty-nine years, people's imaginations were really running wild.

When I regained consciousness from my Rip Van Winkle style–slumber and called the studio, everyone was relieved. It should be noted that I arrived at Studio 1-A with plenty of time to spare. My colleagues were not in danger of not having a weatherperson. There was no chance they'd have to pull a stranger in from off the plaza to fill my shoes. All was well! Nothing to see here, folks! So even though I was on set and ready to go promptly at 7:00 A.M., the entire country would soon know I overslept thanks to *USA Today.* I can still see the news report:

Al Roker oversleeps, misses early show
Today show veteran Al Roker hit the snooze button one too many times Tuesday.

He completely slept through his 6 A.M. early morning show, *Wake Up with Al*, on The Weather Channel. It was his first time ever snoozing through a show.

"After 39 years, it happened," tweeted Roker, 58. "I overslept and missed a show."

He made it in for *Today*, where he was spotted yawning behind the scenes.

Matt Lauer said, "I tweeted out Rip Van Roker, and I'm getting a lot of tweets back saying a lot of people thought it was RIP Al Roker. Read carefully!"

Surely, I am not the only human being who has overslept. However, I may be the only person to oversleep and have it make the papers, even though by that time in my life I had woken up promptly at 3:45 A.M. over two thousand times. I mean, c'mon, give a guy a break!

My wake-up time isn't something I am overly focused on; it's just part of the job. A good portion of America is just waking up as *The Today Show* starts—people are pouring their first cup of coffee, feeding babies, and making lunches in their bathrobes while we've already been up for hours. I admit it seems reasonable that people would be curious about what it's like to get up that early. My very own family still doesn't seem to get it. The running joke come Friday night is "Dad, why are you so tired?" Does my family still not know what I do for a living?

I don't live my life like a drill sergeant. Now that my little kids are grown up, I often sleep until 8:00 A.M. on weekends and holidays. However, naps are to be avoided in my opinion. They mess with my sleep cycle. That being said, I have indeed been known to pass out cold on long flights and car rides (where I am the passenger, obviously). During the week I get up at 3:45 A.M. but theoretically, if I slept until 5:00 A.M. I could still make it—I just might have to get dressed in the car on the way to the studio.

But the reason I've come to love my schedule is that time alone before your day begins in earnest is one of the best gifts you can give yourself. Solitary time is an excellent way to clear your mind. Give your mind time to be open and calm, and watch how problems start to seem less overwhelming and life gets just a little bit easier.

People generally assume that waking up early is the one thing I don't love about my job. "But you're just about to enter your third cycle of REM sleep," they say with their lips curled up in a grimace. But my predawn wake-up hour is a huge positive.

It is amazing what can happen when you allow yourself time to be alone and enjoy some quiet time. I'm not saying you'll be having *Eureka!* moments left and right, but things do come to you if you're receptive. By the way, it doesn't work if you're scrolling through your phone. It's in those peaceful predawn moments where I think about the important things like, You know what would make this Halloween really great? If I erected a giant inflatable Stay Puft Marshmallow Man right in front of the house. Yes. This will add just the right amount of whimsy to our regular Halloween decorating scheme! Or, Huh. Maybe I should try some purple-framed glasses! Mmhmm, I do look quite good in purple. Things come to you when you make the space in your mind. I believe this is the same reason that I've always really enjoyed solitary pursuits in general, like kayaking or biking. If your brain is constantly receiving data, it's hard for any fresh thoughts to make their way past the front door.

A warning! If you get up earlier you may have to stop complaining about never having time to do anything. People love to say, "Oh, I'd exercise/cook/bake/knit/read/learn curling but I just don't have the time!" This is partially because, as most of us know, after a long day at work we generally don't come home bursting with the energy we need to just go ahead and write that screenplay! It's nearly impossible to get anything done at night, and if you are one of those people who writes poetry at 9:00 P.M. and then settles down for a good scrapbooking session—I bow to you.

But don't sell yourself short and not pursue an activity that interests you because you're too tired when you get home. I get it! There's nothing more I'd like to do after dinner than pop on a smoking jacket and some slippers and sink back into a cozy chair with my dog Pepper at my feet and light a pipe.* Getting up early has allowed me to keep a journal. There's nothing better than flipping through a journal and stumbling upon interesting entries I've written such as:

> The men in Paris look so cool. Instead of bulky winter coats they just wear a thicker blazer like corduroy or tweed. They top it off with a cool hat, leather gloves and a big artsy scarf. Dare I attempt this look during a New York winter? These guys look très chic! Leila [my daughter] thinks I should stick to a parka. But c'mon, I think I can make this look work!

Or maybe . . .

---

*My wife would never, ever allow a pipe in the house. But a man can dream!

Made a new chicken dish today. Roasted chicken
with a maple butter sauce. I stuffed the cavity with
rosemary and it was superb. Definitely need to
make this one again!

Sometimes I only write a couple of sentences, sometimes a page or two, but now I have a running record of
what I've done with my life. And exercise is just something
I'd prefer to get out of the way. Exercise is not my favorite activity, but I've accepted it's something that has to be
done should I wish to stay alive. I meet with my trainer,
Don, a few times a week at 4:40 A.M. Exercising at that
hour just gets it out of the way. It's over (thank God), and I
don't have to have any anxiety about when am I going to
exercise for the rest of the day.

Stop the cycle of watching Netflix but kicking yourself
for not getting to that ship in a bottle you've been dying
to build instead. Do yourself a favor—go ahead and watch
Netflix, but commit to getting up earlier tomorrow and
doing whatever it is you want to do. I realize it may seem
daunting to get up earlier.* Who doesn't like the comfort
of a warm bed? We all do—but get over it! When you get

---

*For those of you who struggle to fall asleep at night, I highly rec-
ommend an audio book, ideally a long biography of a dead president. Three minutes of a book like this and I'm out. This may work
for you.

up early there's just you and the clock—your kids aren't asking you for anything, no one at work is asking you to jump into a meeting . . . because they are all asleep! Getting yourself to bed and waking up just one hour earlier offers up a world of options. Whether you're seeking that precious time for yourself, or you want to finally prove to all your friends that, yes, you really can write a novel—that single hour in the morning is golden. It can take you places you'd never thought you'd go.

ALTRUISM #11

Don't Goober Smoocher

FROM THE DICTIONARY of Al Roker:

Goober smoocher (verb): to engage
in conversation for the sole purpose of
impressing people; showing off who you know,
how smart you are, how perfect your children are,
or how superior your next vacation is compared
to the rest of the world's. You get the idea.

I'm terrible at socializing. One of the things I admire most
about Deborah is that she has the gift of smooth conversation. If I hadn't married Deborah, I doubt I would know
anyone or go anywhere—ever. The kids would be out, living full lives, and I'd be sitting at home with my dog Pepper, pondering some of life's biggest questions, many of
which happen to be related to animation.

If Pluto's a dog, what is Goofy? Is he really a dog, or
some doglike creature?
If they're both dogs, how did Goofy evolve
enough to figure out that if he walked on hind legs
and put on pants he could live in a house and drive
a car, while Pluto was still getting his ass kicked
by Chip 'n' Dale? Is he not dog enough? Why the
disparity?

I'm willing to accept that Yogi Bear can talk. But if he's intelligent enough to carry on conversations, why does he wear a tie—but no shirt? That makes no sense whatsoever. Everyone knows a shirt is more comfortable than a tie. Any normal person (or bear?) knows that given a choice you'd choose a shirt over a tie any day.

And perhaps most puzzling, why do so many animated characters only have four fingers? And why in the name of all that is holy are they always wearing gloves? What exactly are they hiding under there? Was the fifth finger lost in a gruesome industrial accident?

The world of animation presents a never-ending series of mysteries for me to ponder alone, at home. But Deborah, she can talk to anyone in any situation. Celine Dion, or Siegfried and Roy in their secret garden with the possibility of white tigers lurking around? No problem, she's cool as a cucumber. Small children, the elderly? She'll effortlessly switch the conversation from stuffed animals to Florida retirement communities. Sure, I can shake hands and engage in a quick hello with folks who come see us on the plaza. People are generally friendly and I appreciate it when people get up early and come by, sometimes even braving the rain or the blazing-hot August sun. But if the producers suddenly rolled out an open bar and servers started walking around with platters of maple-glazed bacon, my heart rate would soar and I'd look for the nearest potted plant to stand behind. Social situations simply do not highlight my strengths as a human being.

Every summer, inevitably, one of my wife's lovely friends invites us to stay at their Hamptons home for the weekend.* In case you aren't up to date on the favorite weekend spots of luminaries such as Diddy and Beyoncé, the Hamptons are where the uber wealthy go to enjoy a relaxing respite at the beach. This can mean anything from hosting an all-white-apparel dinner party with a waterfall of champagne for hundreds of their closest friends in their Gatsbyesque mansion, or standing in line for hours to eat at a restaurant where a Cobb salad is $45.

When I was growing up in Queens, a trip to the beach meant a Ford Country Squire station wagon stuffed with my parents and the six of us kids, warm tuna fish sandwiches sprinkled with a hint of sand no matter how hermetically sealed the Saran wrap was, a hot Coke, and a gritty Rice Krispies treat, if I was lucky. It was on these trips that I developed a fear of any whiff of spoiled food or leftovers. Any mayonnaise-based food that had been in the sun for more than twenty minutes was strictly forbidden.

---

*To my wife's friends: Deborah indeed enjoys her time spent with you in the Hamptons. Continue to invite her! It's not her fault that I am an insufferable anti-snob (well, sometimes).

Once my mother literally slapped a forkful of potato salad out of my sandy little fingers. "Don't eat that! It's been in the sun too long. Now go wait thirty minutes before you go in the water, otherwise your belly will expand and you'll puff up in the water like a blowfish!"

After all that fun, we'd all be packed in the car, covered in sand. Since I was the oldest and we only had one bathroom, I had to wait till my other five sibs were bathed before I got my turn in the shower, which by that time, there was about six inches of sand in the tub. It was a good time on the simplest level. However, nothing about the Hamptons is simple.

Just getting there is nearly impossible. The A-listers arrive by helicopter or seaplane, while non-billionaires are forced to sit in traffic on the Montauk Highway for a decade. Sitting in the car anticipating the time when I'll be able to stretch my legs is torture, and I usually can't help but start to wonder about the fact that if there's only one way in, there's only one way out! Does this not concern anyone at all?

I know a thing or two about hurricanes, and while they don't exactly appear without any prior warning, I definitely wouldn't want to be one of the poor fools who couldn't be whisked out quickly via helicopter. (The thing is I *would be* one of those poor fools, stuck in the car like a sitting duck waiting to be carried off by the storm surge. The irony of a weather forecaster going this way is almost too much.)

Sure, the Hamptons do have a few draws. There are miles upon miles of pristine white sand, classic beach cottages with window boxes overflowing with flowers . . . dotted along the roads between behemoth estates with fourteen chimneys. (Who lights fires in the summer? Much less over a dozen fires?) It's undeniably pretty. And while I object to the traffic and the $18 price tag for a basic gallon of milk, I admit my biggest issue with the Hamptons may very well be myself. Here's the thing: I don't goober smoocher.

I just don't. I do not enjoy conversations about wine vintages, polo, elite skiing resorts, racing cars, or SAT scores. I don't really want to hear about someone's plans to spend Christmas in Bali. It's not how I like to spend my free time. I'd much prefer to be at home, organizing my dress shirts. But because my talented wife also happens to be a very good person, she also supports various charities and foundations by buying tickets to fundraisers. I try to be a good husband, I really do, so I'll agree to go to a handful of events with her each year. I squelch the anxiety I feel as I rip my tuxedo out of the dry cleaner bag anticipating awkward small talk with fancy-pants people. As much as I'm complaining here, Deborah has brought me to a couple of Hamptons parties each year thrown by some really terrific couples who bring together some amazingly unstuffy folks, and I have to confess my attitude is changing. How bad can the beach really be?? Get a grip, Roker!

Socializing, dinner parties, small talk—human interactions of any sort can feel nearly impossible to navigate at times. I am here to tell you that for some of us (I include myself here) this doesn't get any easier with age or confidence. But the good news is that there are ways to manage this. I've learned a few surefire tricks to get through almost any social situation unscathed. After many years of awkward social interactions, I can honestly say that socializing is about survival.

While I have accepted that I will never, ever have easygoing conversational skills like my wife, I have learned a few tactics for getting through these affairs.

Follow the platter.

This works for any event that has food (and if there's no food, why are you even there?). I once went to opening night at the New York City Ballet where there were passed appetizers. Fittingly, the food served at an event celebrating very thin, yet athletic dancers consisted of organic baby grass on gluten-free rounds of nothing. But then I noticed that a large percentage of the men at the event were gathered together in one area of the room. What was going on?

Curiosity got the better of me—were they making bets? Had a fistfight broken out? So I wandered over to see what was up. What was up was a big, beautiful, overflowing silver platter of maple-candied bacon. The platter of bacon was like a siren song, the scent alone luring over the bored and hungry. Someone in charge must've realized the dinner portion wasn't even big enough to satisfy a mouse. Bacon is a damn good reason to attend a party. Whether you're at a neighbor's Christmas party, a work function, or a networking event there's going to be at least one food that is the big standout. You never know what it might be: bacon, Swedish meatballs, lamb chop lollipops, shrimp cocktail, perhaps a casserole covered in cracker crumbs, or a seven-layer dip of some sort. Bottom line, if you find that platter, you're going to have an easier time making it through the event. Trust me.

Work the perimeter.

The hard truth is that 98 percent of people don't care what you have to say. They're scanning the room thinking about who they want to talk to next—who might be more important or more interesting? Who has nine million Instagram followers? And maybe they'll be willing to like my new line of organic edible coffee cups. No way is someone going to engage a weatherperson in conversation if, say, Spike Lee is in the room—and I get it. That guy has some serious accomplishments under his belt. I mean, c'mon! I may hold three Guinness world records, but "longest running weather forecast" pales in comparison to directing a classic film like *Do the Right Thing* or winning an Academy Award for *BlacKkKlansman*. I can't compete! So, I default to working the perimeter of the room. To execute this maneuver, simply stand at the edge of the nearest group of people who are engaged in conversation. Nod your head. Laugh if it seems appropriate. After a few minutes slowly back away. Repeat the process as necessary.

Just stay mute and listen.

As a person who has attended a good deal of functions over the past fifty years or so, listening remains the easiest and most effective tactic for surviving in a social situation. When you find yourself actually engaged in conversation with someone, don't panic! Here's the trick: just let them do all of the talking! The truth is most people want to be listened to. More often than not everyone is trying to get their point heard, trying to share a story about themselves—they're just talking and not listening. When you really listen, you'll find whoever you're talking to will direct the conversation to a place where you can naturally ask a question. When executed properly, this tactic can play out like so:

"Hello, I'm Al, nice to meet you. So, may I ask what is it you do for a living?"

"Of course! I'm an entomologist. That means I work with bugs. I've had a deep passion for insects my entire life."

"Wow, I've never met an entomologist! Do you have a favorite insect?"

"Well, the assassin bug is a fascinating specimen."

"Oh, is it?"

"Indeed. Its mouth can pierce through the exoskeleton of its prey—then it injects a toxin that paralyzes the victim, and then the assassin bug proceeds to liquefy the prey's insides. They've also been known to wear the husks of the creatures they've killed on their backs. Kind of like a sick backpack. You know how serial killers keep trophies? Like that."

"Well, that certainly is interesting!"

"The bug world is more fascinating than you could ever believe. Did you know that the rarest insect on earth is the Dryococelus australis?"

"No. I did not."

"Yes, it's incredibly rare because in 1918, a beat-up British ship had to stop at Lord Howe Island off the eastern coast of Australia for repairs. The ship was only docked there for nine days, but during that time a large group of black rats that had stowed away on the ship escaped onto the island and ate all the bugs. It was believed every last one of them was devoured by the rats. But thankfully a few have been found— the rats didn't eat all of them after all!"

"Really?"

"Yes, and they're so large sometimes they're referred to as 'tree lobsters.'"

"Whoa. Well, it was really nice to meet you. Now, if you'll excuse me, I'm going to go find some bacon to snack on. Have a great evening!"

Do you see how little speaking was required on my part? I barely said a thing in that totally fictional scenario I just relayed to you. I simply asked very basic questions, building on the answers given for each question. The bottom line is the more you listen, the easier it is to ask questions.

While I am not great at socializing, I've come to learn the true value behind really listening. I believe my ability to listen and not have to be the one leading the conversation at all times is another secret behind my success. I've had the great privilege of interviewing many people over the years, and when you just listen—people open up.

On my program *Cold Cuts with Al Roker* on *Today*'s YouTube channel, I invite people to come on the show and we chat, and they tell me about their favorite sandwiches. You wouldn't believe how people open up when you're just piling on cured meats and cheeses. I interviewed the classic comedy duo known as Cheech & Chong and before I asked a single question, Cheech admitted he was named after a pork rind, and then Chong demonstrated the knife skills he learned in prison. To be clear, the knife skills did not relate to warfare of any kind but pertained to how to perfectly slice an onion. Had I been blathering on about the fine qualities of Havarti cheese versus a sharp cheddar, there's a good chance I wouldn't have gotten this great life tidbit. In the end, listening always works.

Don't feel anxious the next time you're faced with a daunting social situation. Remember, most people who make small talk at an event survive. Just get through it the best you can. As great as it would be if we could all stay home in our slippers, making it through life as a human being requires socialization from time to time. If you want to have friends, excel at work, learn new things, or stay married, chances are you're going to occasionally talk to a person who is a complete stranger or who you barely know. Don't stress about making small talk, just get through it. Nod your head, ask questions, listen, and if all else fails simply resort to this gem: "What's your favorite sandwich?"

ALTRUISM #12

Unless You're *Literally*
the Sun, Work Doesn't
Revolve Around You

IF YOU WERE TO ASK ME, "Al, however did you go from a local weekend weather forecaster to the weatherperson on *The Today Show? The Today Show* is a big deal! You've been on it for years—you're basically a national treasure! Pray tell, how did you do it?"

If this conversation were to take place in my massive corner office in Rockefeller Center, I'd lean back in my chair and put my feet up on my gold-plated desk (which is the length of a football field). I'd offer you a brandy from a decanter made out of diamonds and have my cigar butler roll a stogie for you. Then I'd explain quite simply that I got my first big break, the weekday local weather job, after challenging the great Frank Field to a duel. Why wait for a promotion or a job opening when you can ask someone to engage in a fight-to-the-death match?

"I'm happy to tell you, but first, can I offer you a caviar blini? I have them imported from Russia daily. Or would you like my personal chef to prepare you something else? An omelet perhaps? They keep a flock of chickens for me on the roof should I have a hankering for a fresh egg. Or maybe you'd prefer one of those popular grain bowls with handpicked farro? Okay, *The Today Show*, you asked? How did that happen? Well, I adored Willard Scott, as you know; he's like a second father to me. But, occasionally I'd trick him into calling in sick by getting him front-row seats to the circus. Then voila! Roker is here to fill in . . . *conveniently.*"

Then you'd watch as I tilted my head back and laughed (maniacally, of course). And because you now know I have complete control over the weather—the sky would darken, illuminated by a flash of lightning and punctuated with a crack of thunder.

Then I'd explain that I offered to take my beloved mentor to lunch one day at the finest restaurant in all of Manhattan. We had spaghetti and steak. When our car pulled up, I put a bag over Willard's head, then shoved him in the car in which he was driven to a secret airfield in Queens and flown to a lovely split-level ranch home I had prepared for him in Idaho.

Well, no one had any idea where Willard was. The producers and management looked all over—he wasn't at the circus, in the break room, or hanging out in the Rainbow Room drinking Manhattans and eating shrimp cocktail anymore. But obviously the weather doesn't stop just because a weatherperson is missing! It had all come down to me to save the show. So, I ordered a giant cake (the kind from the 1950s that had room for a stripper inside). I got in the cake and had an NBC page roll me out onto the set at precisely 7:00 A.M. (I had slipped him a $20 bill and a ham sandwich—those kids are flat broke.) Katie Couric and Bryant Gumbel, who were the hosts at the time, were a little puzzled by the sight of a massive chocolate cake that was starting to melt under the heat of the lights. Katie said, "Who did this? It's not my birthday!" But then I popped out of it! The page blew one of those weird long trumpets used to announce royalty and I said:

> Citizens of America! From today hence, I,
> Albert Lincoln Roker, will forecast the weather on
> NBC's *Today Show* forever, and ever and ever!

Oddly, but conveniently, Katie had confetti in her purse, which she gleefully tossed around, and Bryant was so happy he burst into tears. Then we had a ticker-tape parade down Fifth Avenue. And that is how I got my job on *The Today Show*!

If you're googling the contact information for the FBI right now, relax. No one was killed, kidnapped, or even tricked into going to the circus along the career path of Al Roker. However, had I told you how it really went down it's possible I would have bored you to death.

The truth is, my journey probably isn't that different than anyone else's. And my office at 30 Rock? It can comfortably seat two people (other than me) or three if they are diet deficient enough to smush themselves together in my old plaid love seat I brought in from home. My office's most notable features are a decent-sized window (yay!), my collection of stuffed animals, my framed certificate from the American Meteorological Society, and the treadmill desk my wife bought me so I can nail those ten thousand daily steps rather than keeling over and dying. If I'm meeting with someone in my office, I can offer them an individual-sized bag of bacon-cheddar-flavored Whisps and a bottle of Poland Spring—both of these items can be found at Costco.

My job is on TV, sure—but ultimately I got to where I am today by being patient, working hard, and showing up every day to do the best job I could. And occasionally being in the right place at the right time.

Not even a year after I took that less than perfect job doing the weekend weather at WNBC, Frank Field got into a contract dispute and went over to WCBS, where he continued to thrive. Since I was doing well with the weekend weather, I was then given the full-time gig. There is a bonus when you are the weatherperson on New York City's local NBC channel—just by the nature of proximity you get tapped to do the national weather on *The Today Show*. This was because the studios are conveniently located about a one-minute elevator ride away from each other. If Willard was out on assignment or out on vacation and they needed a body—I was right there! It's the same to this day. If I'm on vacation, and Dylan is out sick, one of our producers will call WNBC's Dave Price or Janice Huff. Dave and Janice are great, but their availability and proximity make them amazing.

I would continue to fill in for my dear friend Willard for a few years. Eventually Willard's schedule changed; Fridays off (drop in Al Roker!), Mondays and Fridays off (again, put Roker in there!).

When Willard retired and I took over in January of 1996, most people didn't even notice. By March though, folks apparently started to get sick of my face because everyone was suddenly asking . . . "Hey. Where is Willard? Why is Roker here all the time?" And it was with all of this fanfare that I started my full-time career at *The Today Show.*

See, there were no dramatic moments or big cause for celebration. No dramas or entourage. It'll probably make for a good bedtime story for my future grandchildren.

I have worked at NBC for ages, and throughout the years there was never any guarantee that I would land where I did. Willard could have continued doing the weather longer, they could have found a slimmer version of me, the cards could have fallen in many different ways. But I didn't focus on what the end of the road looked like. I was concerned about doing my job to the best of my ability and enjoying my career at whatever stage it was at.

I am well aware that my job comes with many enjoyable side effects—travel, access, good money, and meeting fascinating people—but at the end of the day it's still a job (yes, I know it's a very good one). But no matter where you work, your typical day-to-day isn't going to be all giant chocolate cakes and bacon bouquets. The majority of the work we do on *The Today Show* is not glamorous. We all have work to do, meetings to attend, phone calls to return, emails to write, and we often work long hours.

I KNOW IT'S UNPLEASANT when work interferes with regular life. Those times when you're missing something that's really important to you like your sister's birthday party, or even your parent's big anniversary cruise. Sure, that's a bummer, but that is the nature of work. Work is not based around your personal obligations and needs. Your employers will rarely give you a cake for all of your accomplishments.

Work can feel completely impossible at times. I mean, I'd love to take off every other Wednesday for a massage and facial, but that's not how *work* works. You're being paid to do something and that means you do it. I have to be where? At what time? And then get to the other side of the country to do what? You want me to break a Guinness world record by doing the weather for how many consecutive hours? Sometimes I'd look at that trusty old Filofax of mine and see the solid wall of tasks, commitments, and travel plans and I couldn't help but think, if I didn't love this Filofax so much, I'd consider throwing it out of my office window right now. Take that, obligations and commitments! But then I'd take a breath and get a grip.

I am blessed with a job that goes above and beyond anything a guy like me could have imagined having. When you're overwhelmed, take a breath—give yourself a minute, but for God's sake get back at it, because in the end you never know where it can take you.

ALTRUISM #13

*You Don't Need to Be
the Top Banana*

FROM THE DICTIONARY of Al Roker:

Top banana (noun): the person at the top of
the pecking order. The top banana has the
biggest job, which while prestigious and impressive
is accompanied by relentless work responsibilities
and massive amounts of pressure. Being top
banana may or may not directly impact the level
of silliness you are allowed to exhibit on a day-to-
day basis, especially if you work in live television.

Years ago I got to interview Ed McMahon, Johnny Carson's forever sidekick, at his sprawling 1930s Mediterra-
nean-style mansion in Bel Air. Ed greeted me on one of
the *two terraces* off the back of the house that offered a
sweeping view of Century City.

I marveled at the long pool flanked by graceful Greek
columns. "Nice pool, Ed!"

He looked at me. "What, oh you meant that fountain?"
Ohhhhhh.

The real pool shimmered brightly off the side of the
property and looked like it could comfortably contain all
of Los Angeles.

While the camera crew was setting up for the interview,
Ed gave me a tour of the interior of his home. It felt like

we were walking through the museum of broadcasting. As he guided me through a series of never-ending rooms, Ed pointed out pictures of himself with athletes, movie stars, and presidents. He might have been best known for saying *"Here's Johnny,"* but he parlayed the fame that came from sitting next to the biggest late-night star in the world into a successful career as both a commercial pitchman and TV star in his own right. The setup was always the same—Johnny behind the desk, the star in the chair next to Johnny, the guest (maybe Don Rickles or Rodney Dangerfield [again, ask your parents]), and then Ed. Ed was always just one seat away, because Johnny was the real star of the show after all. "I've made peace with the fact that I wasn't the star. Johnny was the star."

Ed went on to explain that his role still gave him proximity and access to greatness. He sat one seat away from some of the biggest movie, television, and Broadway stars. Looking around his beautiful home, it was safe to say that Ed had enjoyed a very successful career.

Willard echoed a similar sentiment one day. "Al, we do the weather and that gives us second-banana status. There's nothing wrong with being the second banana. I mean, I think the second banana is a pretty sweet deal! You can build a really successful career and not let it take over your entire life! There's less pressure! You don't need to know who every congressman is, or who are the senators of South Dakota."

After sharing this great bit of career and life advice, it wouldn't have been at all unusual for Willard to take off his toupee, toss it haphazardly in a desk drawer, and put on a Carmen Miranda fruit hat before doing the weather forecast. See! Second bananas have all the fun!

I am not the top banana at *The Today Show*, and this is a beautiful thing as far as I'm concerned. Co-hosts Savannah and Hoda are the Top Bananas. They are the captains who steer the ship and they are the face of the broadcast. Both of these ladies are serious, tough journalists. Between the two of them, these fierce women have interviewed presidents, senators, presidential candidates, celebrities, icons, and giants of industry. They've covered the toughest topics with grace: Sandy Hook, the war in Iraq, Hurricane Katrina, and the Boston Marathon bombing to name just a few. And I know I play a big role on the show, especially as record-breaking high temperatures, deadly heat waves, fires, massive flooding, and hurricanes have meant that weather and climate change are bigger newsmakers than ever before. The weather sometimes takes the top-banana news status if you will. But, ultimately, while they let me interview the occasional celebrity, I'm not the news guy. I don't interview the big newsmakers (the politicians, analysts, and pundits) and that's fine.

I've always fancied myself to be the George Wendt of *The Today Show*. To refresh your memory, Wendt played

Norm, the bar regular/accountant on the hit television show *Cheers* that ran for over a decade.

Norm's character is the pleasant, warm and fuzzy guy who people are generally happy to see. When Wendt's character entered the bar, everyone would shout out "Norm!" Then he'd take his usual seat at the bar and order a beer that was added to his never-ending tab. Wendt had at least one really great line on each show:

"How's life treating you, Norm?"

"Like it's a dog-eat-dog world out there, and I'm wearing Milk-Bone underwear."

Or

"How's a beer sound, Norm?"

"I dunno. I usually finish them before they get a word in."

Ba-da-bing! Wendt delivered some great zingers, and he was nominated for six Emmys for outstanding supporting actor too. All of that sounds like big success to me, even though there were bigger bananas on the show. It doesn't matter that you're not the star; it matters that you're *part of the constellation.* Dream big, set huge goals, and by all means have great expectations for yourself, but know that you don't have to reach the very, very top to be considered a success. In fact, there's something to be said about being the second banana. You can forge your own trails and create your own narrative without the strictures of being the top banana. If it so happens that you are at a place in your career where you're not the top banana, I say embrace it!

It's a great place to be for several reasons, and one of them is that the second banana is basically granted permission to avoid putzes! We get all kinds of people as guests on *The Today Show*. You never really know who you might encounter walking around Studio 1-A. A reality-show star, an athlete, a pop star with an entourage comprised of eighty-six absolutely essential people (give or take a dozen or so). I will start by saying that 99.9 percent of our guests are just delightful when in our space. And, sure, it's thrilling to walk into the studio and run into celebrities I admire, but there are also people who come on the show who are not the nicest of folks. When there is someone on who is a real putz, I can either (a) shake their hand, say "nice to meet you," and end the conversation right then and there or (b) make an about-face and leave the studio immediately.

Now, you may be wondering, Al, what's a putz? Hang on a second, I've got you. According to the Merriam-Webster dictionary, informally, (1) "a stupid, foolish, or ineffectual person" and (2) a "penis." Take your pick.

So, WHEN PEOPLE come on *Today* they are expecting to meet the co-hosts. No celebrity/politician/rock star/person of note is ever sitting in the greenroom enjoying a sparkling water and packet of dry-roasted almonds thinking, Wait a minute. Why hasn't the weatherperson come by and introduced himself to me? I demand the weatherperson be brought forth to me at once!

Nor are any of the powers that be thinking, Where is Roker? He should be here to make an introduction! Roker should be here shaking hands! No one is focused on the second banana, and in cases like this it is a real blessing.

And try being second banana at home. The reminders that I'm a second banana are plentiful around the Roker household—I can't even avoid them when I cook.

I like to cook. I find it relaxing to chop vegetables and sear meats all in the name of preparing a delicious dinner for my family. The act of slicing an onion and the sound of a piece of meat sizzling on a hot pan relax me. When I plate a meal and set it down on the table and join my family to eat, I know all is about right with the world. Roasted chicken, shrimp salad, maybe a seared loin of lamb. These are the simple pleasures in life that make everything worthwhile.

In my kitchen at our home in New York, I try to keep fresh fruits and vegetables on hand. It's possible I'll keep delicious apples from upstate New York on the counter. Maybe I'll even put them in a nice bowl, trying to create the illusion of a Martha Stewart–style domestic bliss. But in order to achieve that look, I have to move various papers off the counter including–The Binder.

I am married to a seasoned journalist who brings home a gigantic binder full of the information she needs to get ready for an interview. The Binder sitting right there on the counter is the clearest evidence I can think of as to how different the preparation is for a top banana versus a second banana. The Binder looks like the kind of thing someone would drag around if they were planning to program a supercomputer at NASA circa 1965. The Binder is daunting. It features sections divided up with color-coded tabs. I've never dared open one of my wife's binders, but I imagine it to be full of charts, graphs, diagrams, perhaps even secret codes. There could be a scratch-and-sniff section for all I know, as the top banana Deborah needs to be incredibly prepared for her interviews. She must convey accurate information to the public about current events or newsmakers, and that often means asking tough questions.

As a second banana who interviews fun people like Sir Paul McCartney, Ringo Starr, and Eddie Murphy, I am bringing home a slim file at best. That's because I am generally interviewing people who had a fairly cemented presence in the world before I ever showed up to interview them. I'm hoping to give people a glimpse inside their lives, not discuss who they think is likely to win the Nobel Prize for mathematics next year. People are more curious about things like a celebrity's favorite breakfast foods, or if they prefer dogs over cats.

Sometimes the folder contains a single piece of paper, leading me to believe it is placed in the file to make me feel better about myself. Here's Roker's one paragraph of notes for his upcoming interview. I guess they put it in a file to create a sense of importance, or suggest that he has real work to do? Or maybe they know I'm prone to spilling things on important documents?

I've been at NBC for more than forty years. Forty years, for God's sake! The odds of anyone being the top banana for that long are frankly on the low side. Who can sustain that level of intensity for such a long period of time? A good supporting role can keep you going for a very long time. No one is gunning to be the second banana—your position is safe! While reaching your highest goals is a wonderful thing, know that you can still make a strong impact as a second banana.

And by the way, no one has ever said that you'll never be the first banana. While you're cast in the role of second banana, you're honing all of your skills. Someday, if you are called to the very top of the banana hierarchy, you'll be ready to slide right into that role. But here's the thing— if that call never comes? That's okay too. It's a good thing to make peace with this. It's important to accept your accomplishments and the success you've enjoyed, even if it isn't exactly what you thought it would be. Okay, it may not be what you want, but take it from a guy who has been second banana for decades—while you're waiting for what you want, don't miss out on all the good things you already have. It really has an amazing a-peel!!! Come on, I waited till the end to slip that one in . . . yeah, that one too.

ALTRUISM #14

Don't Freak Out

I WAS SCHEDULED to take the road test for my driver's license that afternoon, so my dad was going to take me out in the ole Country Squire station wagon for some last-minute practice.

The Roker family car was an absolutely enormous vehicle, turd-brown, featuring a steering wheel as hard as concrete, lap belts, and flip-back seats in the rear that faced the traffic (where the youngest usually sat; those kids would have been guava jelly if the car was hit from behind). When the Roker family went on a Sunday drive back in the 1960s or '70s, they were taking their lives in their own hands. The safety features in cars were so lacking back then that we might as well have been climbing Mount Everest without oxygen.

AS A BUS DRIVER, Dad knew that driving anywhere in New York City was like going to war. You had to be ready for anything. You couldn't just sit back, casually dangling your arm out the open window while singing along to Earth, Wind & Fire. There's an insane traffic battle out there, and New York City drivers are very aggressive. A typical drive in the city will likely include a near miss with another car or maybe being cut off by a massive speeding bus. In addition to nearly *being* killed, it is almost impossible not to nearly kill someone else, with pedestrians stepping directly into your path or a bicycle delivery person shooting through a traffic light at breakneck speed. *(For God's sake, you will survive if your pad thai isn't delivered to your door within six minutes of placing the order. Can we agree that bicycle delivery people should be allowed to ride at a reasonable speed?!)* And there's no point in honking your horn these days; no one will hear you. People are too busy walking and text-messaging and they can't hear anything! They are listening to their favorite true-crime podcasts, wrapped up in a murder mystery that could very well be their own, but they are oblivious!

But back when I was learning to drive, the horn was actually useful—using it was an art form. The polite tap on the horn signaled *Hey you, I'm here and I'm not convinced you see me.* The full-on, extended blare of the horn signaled: *Thanks for cutting me off, you moron* or *Brace yourself for impact!*

Dad was determined that I be prepared for my driver's test. So, we started off well. I eased the car out of park, lightly put my foot on the pedal, and went less than twenty driving right past a cemetery, where I saw my own demise flash before my eyes as I sailed by in the steel-death-box-on-wheels. But I was careful with the brake like Dad said; I didn't want his coffee flying through the front window shield. I successfully executed a lane change, and the sweat that had been accumulating on my forehead was now freely leaking into my eyes. I kept driving at the speed limit without crashing into anyone or anything. Dad said, "You seem about ready for the big test." I exhaled.

Just as we were pulling up to the house, Dad said, "Al, one more thing. How's your broken U-turn? Let's do one before we go to the DMV." I take a deep breath and turn back to make sure the street is clear, execute the first part of the turn flawlessly but then suddenly we're moving forward. What! We are moving forward and we're picking up speed! Suddenly I am completely disoriented and don't know what's happening. My body temperature has gone up about a hundred degrees and I can't get any words out of my mouth to ask what I am doing wrong! What's happening to the car?! "Brake-brake-brake," Dad says, staring straight ahead as cool as a cucumber. But suddenly I don't know what a brake is! What's a brake?! "Brake-brake-brake," he repeats like a mantra. When my brain finally receives the message that my foot is on the gas pedal and not the brake, we've careened clear across the Vereens' front lawn, stopping about two inches short of their front stoop.

I take a quick look around and assess the carnage. I've torn up Mr. Vereen's meticulously cared for grass and uprooted one of his beloved azaleas. Surveying the destruction, I'm scared to look over at my dad. *Will I even live to see tomorrow?* As sweat begins to bead on my forehead, I finally look up at Dad. He's sitting in the passenger seat looking as serene as the Dalai Lama.

"Okay, Al. Let's back up and try it again."

What? "You want me to try it again? I just killed grass, an azalea bush, and had a very close encounter with a brick stoop!"

"Al, just back up. You're going to do it again. We can fix all of this." I take a breath and I get back out onto the road, and letting my dad's voice calm my nerves, I pull off the maneuver.

"Good job, Al. There's just one thing I need to do before we go to your test."

My dad reached into the glove compartment and pulled out an old envelope and rooted around until he found a pen.

Mr. Vereen:
Sorry about the mess we made with your lawn.
Al had some trouble with that broken U-turn.
We'll be back to fix the damage just a bit later.
I'm taking Al for his driver's test.
Albert Roker

My dad got out of the car, walked across what was left of the neighbor's lawn, and tucked the note behind the storm door. He climbed back in and said, "Let's go, time to take your test." While I was terrified of being grounded, never being allowed to drive, and subject to the wrath of my neighbor whose lawn I had just ruined, my dad stayed completely calm.

"Aren't you worried about the lawn? Won't we get in trouble with Mr. Vereen?"

"Al, it's all going to be fine, trust me."

Dad wasn't mad at all; he understood the reality of the situation. He knew I did not get behind the wheel of the car thinking, You know what? It would be really fun to destroy our neighbors' landscaping! I'm going to tear up their lawn with this Country Squire station wagon!

It was an honest mistake, and anger would do absolutely nothing to improve the situation. Dad knew there was no point in making me feel worse than I already did. And if he had gotten angry and yelled, threatening to never let me use the Country Squire, he'd be stuck driving me and my siblings around town for years. If I got my license (and wasn't too terrified to drive) he was gaining a chauffeur.

For the record, we made it to the DMV without incident, and I made it through my test with no problem. And it should be noted that I was not asked to execute a broken U-turn during the test.

The kindness and reserve my dad modeled for me is something I tap into nearly every single day of my life, especially when I walk out onto the plaza at 7:30 A.M. I toss out my signature phrase, "And here's what happening in your neck of the woods," to signal the local stations that it's time for their forecast. It's cold out sometimes, so I grab my hat and wrap my scarf around my neck. I step outside and am immediately boosted by the friendly cheers and greetings from the crowd. The plaza is one of my favorite things about *The Today Show*. People are generally happy and excited to be there, holding up their signs and waving to folks back home. How can this not put a smile on a guy's face? We are always grateful people show up because our audience is like part of the cast—what would the show be without our viewers? Several sad, needy people blathering on about current events to no one at all.

I make my way around the crowd, shaking hands, taking selfies, and chatting. I'm moving along when a viewer shakes my hand, looks me directly in the eye, and says, "You look so much better in person!"

I respond, "Why thank you!" as I move onto the next person who wants a selfie.

I get that so often that I've made it the title of this book about my career. I'd like to take a moment to unpack this (as they like to say on cable news).

On a daily basis I have to try to ignore the fact that this comment suggests . . . what? Sometimes when people say this they put a really strong emphasis on "sooooooo," dragging it out in a manner that suggests they're relieved for the sake of all mankind that I don't actually walk around in broad daylight, scaring small children and babies, and traumatizing the fine citizens of New York City with my face. I think people *really think* this is, in fact, a compliment. There are probably frantic texts being sent all over the country . . . citizens of Oklahoma, California, Wisconsin, and Atlanta are waking up to messages from friends on the plaza:

> Guess what? We can all sleep much better at night now because it turns out Al Roker looks so much better in person! It turns out he's not a gargoyle! He doesn't really spend his spare time perched high atop an office building in New York City scowling over the unsuspecting populace!

How do people expect me to respond to this? So, while it's possible I'd like to respond by saying, "Well, for your information that's not actually a compliment. In fact, madam, your offensive comment clearly falls under the category of insults! And good day to you!" I do not say it. Call me a cheeseball* if you will, but I am a little bit old school. Sure, I favor fedoras, fountain pens, stationery, double-breasted suits, family dinners, and old-fashioned hardcover books with actual pages. And, yes, my entire family mocks me for wearing a sports coat on international

---

*While it's true that I don't want to be told I look so much better in person, I am totally fine with "cheeseball."

flights. (Sure, there's a time and place for my beloved and well-worn SUNY Oswego sweatshirts, but it's certainly not while traveling aboard a jet airliner! Have some class!)

But I'm also a big believer in manners, common courtesy, and the golden rule. The one that says "Do unto others as you'd have them do unto you." For this reason, I choose to respond with a thank you—with graciousness—because ultimately I know no harm was meant and no one shows up at *The Today Show* plaza looking to be schooled in manners by a weatherperson (that's actually what this book is for)! I also think the world would be a better place if we all embraced graciousness.

To be clear, I'm not suggesting we all lie down and let the world run us over. This isn't about being naïve or a victim. If necessary, I can get as nuts as the next guy. But how does that ever help in the end? My dad knew that how you react not only reveals something about who you really are but it also has the power to change the situation. You have the choice to react positively or negatively. I admit this isn't always easy either.

Because of my work I am a recognizable person. This is a blessing, and in the age of nine million cable channels, unlimited streaming choices, and countless YouTube videos it's a miracle anyone has any idea who I am. But it's not unusual to run into *The Today Show* viewers in the produce department at the grocery store who want to say hello and take a selfie, and I'm okay with this! But sometimes, after an especially long day, it's possible that I just want to buy some squash and make my way home. But I choose my reaction, which I hope is one of grace and friendliness.

Willard Scott once told me that our viewers are our customers—and we all know the customer is always right.

But what about those of you who may not be on TV or asked for selfies regularly while grocery shopping? Let's be honest for a second. In our hyperwired society where we are often anonymous online, it's never been easier to be mean. Any trolling I've experienced has been limited to the Wild West that is Twitter and Instagram—never once have I been walking down the street minding my own business and had someone approach me and say, "Hey, Al Roker. Yeah you. You suck! And your weather forecasting is rotten!"

But on the internet, people are more bold—once I received a tweet that suggested I look like a "deflated balloon." (I'm sixty-five! Any wrinkles on this face qualify as *character*.) Really, is that the best people can do? Once I was pushed a little further when someone tweeted at me:

> @AlRoker If it rains today, I'm going to punch you on your mouth.

Oh really? You want a piece of me? I've got some news for you, pal. I'm not a wizard. I'm not standing in the basement of Rockefeller Center wearing a velvet cloak, chanting, and waving around a magic wand to coax thunder and lightning from the heavens. But I've got to say, if I did have that power I would have made it rain just for that guy. But because I do not actually control the weather and therefore could not pull revenge precipitation from the sky, I had to settle for dropping my preplanned comeback line:

Go ahead and try it, I will drop you like a bag of dirt.

I first witnessed the power of a truly fantastic comeback line in a most unexpected place—a bookstore. I was on tour for one of my earlier books and my publisher had paired me with a publicist who was present at all the events. She was a very kind, very polite young woman who had grown up in the South. Her manners were impeccable, her appearance neat—if she had pulled a pitcher of sweet tea and a platter of fresh-baked buttermilk biscuits out of her purse I wouldn't have been the least bit surprised. She was pleasant and diligent, she got me where I needed to be on time, and generally made sure things were running smoothly. At the end of the tour I had one last bookstore visit before I headed to the airport to catch a flight back to New York. Time was of the essence, and a pretty big crowd had shown up to have books signed.

I was introduced to the store manager, and she walked us over to where the signing table was set up. Everything appeared to be in order. Fresh Sharpies and a glass of water, check! You can really work up a good thirst signing books. I was ready to go. But then Ms. Publicist's* eyes were drawn to several boxes sitting just a few feet away from the table. The southern congeniality vanished from her face and was replaced with a stone-cold stare. I swear the temperature in the room dropped at least ten degrees when she suddenly shouted out:

Sweet candy Jesus on a milk chocolate cross!

The entire bookstore was silent—even the babies and toddlers who were there for story hour were quiet and waiting to see what would happen. She followed this statement with "With all due respect, what in the F#&k are you thinking, ma'am?" I was terrified but really impressed by how she managed to drop a "ma'am" in there. Like, *I just told you to F#&k off—but it's okay because I called you ma'am.* Wow. This woman was a force. The color drained from the store manager's face as Ms. Publicist continued: "How in the hell do you expect Mr. Roker to sign hundreds

---

*I regret that I am unable to recall my publicist's name on that long ago book tour—but I've never forgotten you!

of books in the time allotted if you haven't pre-flapped them?" Before I could say "Dixie Carter!" a flurry of activity took place. The books were promptly removed from their boxes, the front flaps of the jackets were tucked in just a way that I wouldn't have to flip through the pages to find the blank ones I was supposed to sign. This maneuver apparently would save precious seconds, adding up to the difference between me making my flight and having to sign books well after the bookstore closed.

While I stand by my commitment to old-fashioned manners, the truth is—sometimes people push us right over the edge. I believe in being ready for these moments, and that's why you must arm yourself with a great comeback line.

I stole mine from Julia Louis-Dreyfus. In a *Seinfeld* episode, Elaine and Mr. Costanza are arguing when Mr. Costanza says, "You want a piece of me?" Elaine shuts it all right down by simply saying, "I will drop you like a bag of dirt." Because that's what you do with a dirty, heavy bag of dirt—you *drop it* and walk away. Game over!

You've got to find a line that's satisfying to you, something you know would make you feel superior should you ever have a run-in with a class-A bozo. Years went by before I had an occasion to use my comeback line, and that's fine! It's empowering just knowing it's there.

While it's good to keep that line in your back pocket, ideally it will never have to see the light of day. Graciousness is about kindness, but also about having a generous spirit and disposition, which often means just letting things go.

It does not escape me that I have used this book as an opportunity to rant about the noncompliment I receive on the regular; however, I believe graciousness is also about making your workplace/home/community/school better for everyone. By just saying thank you when someone anti-compliments me, I ultimately hope that I'm helping create a positive and memorable experience for them during their visit to the plaza. In some circumstances, it's better to let things go rather than share your feelings about absolutely everything (unless you are granted the privilege of writing a book, in which case–vent away!).

We all have our own personal versions of *you look so much better in person*–that little life annoyance that could really eat away at you if you let it.

It could be that co-worker who chews too loudly, the friend who just can't stop referring back to that hideous haircut you had in high school, or the boss who can't resist a corny joke with you as the butt of it. Just the thought of it can make you want to scream in frustration. I get it, because I swear I look the same in person, I really do. I mean c'mon, people! But rather than make a federal case out of it, take a moment to think about how you really want to respond. What will your reaction say about you? Are you going to be the guy who yells and screams, creating an epic drama, or are you going to take a breath and gently drive that station wagon that's about the size of Vermont off your neighbor's lawn? The choice is yours. Not freaking out is always an option, and it's usually the best one.

ALTRUISM #15

*Never Say No
and Say Yes*

I T'S NEARLY 7:00 A.M. and the studio is a madhouse of last-minute preparations before we go live. Savannah and Hoda take their places at the big desk—their scripts are in order and they're ready to open the show with the day's breaking news stories. The first thing I do is make sure my phone is on silent (my family has a tendency to call or text me *while I'm on the air* . . . how they still don't understand what I do for a living is beyond me). Once I'm sure my phone is silenced I straighten my tie, adjust my pocket square, and I'm ready to go. Right before I'm about to step onto the set, there it is. That familiar feeling. Nerves! I still get nervous before I go on the air every single morning.

In fact, if the day ever comes when I don't feel that familiar twinge of anxiety, I'm out! I'll walk right out of the studio and head home to begin a life of bingo games and coupon clipping. While I have no plans for retirement whatsoever (even if others think I should), it's that brush with nervousness every morning that signals I'm part of this legendary broadcast. I'm still coming into people's homes, providing the weather, and also some familiar warmth and a smile. *The Today Show* is still exactly where I want to be.

I believe the secret to staying excited about walking into this building after all these years is that I never let things get too familiar. If I got too comfortable, I'd get stale. Who wants to hear about the chances of snow from a dull-eyed, monotone robot. That's what the Weather Channel is for. *I'm kidding.* Really. But if you see a forecast like this from me one morning on *The Today Show,* you should drop everything and write to the powers that be at NBC that Roker needs to go!

I once had the pleasure of interviewing William Shatner. At the age of eighty-eight he is more relevant than ever. When I asked him his secret he said, "I say yes to everything. I say yes to every opportunity that comes my way."

I tried to hide the disappointment on my face, because saying yes is contrary to everything I believe in! I want to say NO. But then I started to think about some of the people I admire most in the entertainment business: Shatner, Tony Danza, and Jeff Goldblum. They're all change artists. After a very successful television career, Danza became a high school English teacher, and now he has a cabaret show. Is this why *he's the boss?* Jeff Goldblum has starred in blockbuster movies like *Jurassic Park*—but he has a band on the side! I love the Mildred Snitzer Orchestra so much that I took my bride to see them perform at the swanky Carlyle Hotel on our anniversary. While saying yes goes against my nature, I don't want to dry up like an old raisin, so I vowed to be open to new opportunities like these guys.

One afternoon I was walking on the treadmill in my office when I got a call from one of the agents in the theatrical division of William Morris Endeavor, David Kalodner. David represents some of the biggest names on Broadway, so naturally I assumed he was calling me by mistake.

So when he said, "The producers of the Broadway musical *Waitress* would like you to be in the show," I was wowed.

"Really, they want me? I can only assume they want me to play the part of Dr. Jim Pomatter, the obstetrician and dashing romantic lead?" I heard a snicker.

"Oh, no. Ha, Al, you're so funny," he said. Why was he laughing? I didn't make a joke. "Actually, they want you to play Old Joe. He's the grumpy elderly man who runs the town diner specializing in pie."

So, it wasn't the romantic lead, but truth be told I do feel a kinship to a good diner, and pie. And it's also true that I had been Broadway-curious for some time. Once I got to make a cameo in *The Will Rodgers Follies* and I got to share the stage with Marla Maples. I also did a guest stint in *The Play What I Wrote*, and was even interviewed by Jiminy Glick, the character played by Martin Short in his one-man Broadway run. And many moons ago, I had been approached by producers to play a role in *The Drowsy Chaperone*. I was informed that the role would essentially entail sitting in a chair on stage and reading from a book. That certainly sounded well suited to my particular talents. But alas, this wasn't meant to be. My mom got seriously sick and I wanted to devote all of my attention to her. She died just three months later and I'm glad I spent that time with her.

Nearly a decade had gone by since my near Broadway experience, and there had been no other offers. I didn't want to let this opportunity slip by, but a musical? Do they understand I'm a weather forecaster? Are they under the impression I can sing and dance?

Before I could respond David said, "Al, why don't you just go to the show and see what you think." Fair enough.

I went to a performance with my daughter Leila. Leila went to LaGuardia High School, a visual arts and performing arts high school in New York City. You may know it as The FAME School, where everyone ran around wearing leg warmers and leotards and spontaneously bursting into song. This school is so famous for pumping out freakishly talented humans like Eartha Kitt, Ben Vereen, Diahann Carroll, and Liza Minnelli, to name just a few, that Alan Parker directed a movie about it in 1980 aptly called *Fame*.

What I'm saying is that they don't mess around at LaGuardia High School. My daughter knows real talent when she sees it. The show was delightful, and all of the actors were fantastic. The musical numbers were terrific too. Ultimately the Old Joe role wasn't the most taxing. This wasn't Victoria in *Cats* we're talking about here—no white unitards or split jumps required. Old Joe made five appearances on stage and sang one song. Could I really do this? After the curtain closed Leila turned to me and said, "Well, Dad. I suppose you could just talk on key."

Good point, dear daughter, which speaks volumes to how you felt about my lullabies all those toddler years.

"Dad. They're asking you to be on Broadway. How can you say no?"

Leila was absolutely right. This was a time to say yes. I was excited about this new venture, but I had two serious concerns:

1. **Totally embarrassing myself.** This was a genuine concern, as I have never sung publicly in my life. Not even karaoke! Would I wake up the next morning after my first performance to discover that the front page of the *Daily News* had a big picture of my face with a headline reading "Category Five Disaster: Al Roker's horrifying Broadway performance has audience members running for safety."

My colleagues at *Today* are generally very supportive and would likely come see the show. If my performance was terrible, things could get really awkward at work. What if I was so bad that Savannah, Hoda, and Craig couldn't even look me in the eye? I had visions of being the office pariah— snubbed at the water cooler.

2. Being a class-A jerk. I knew what a fantastic opportunity performing on Broadway would be, and I couldn't imagine what it would be like to be honing your craft for years, putting in the work, going to all the auditions—only to have a weatherperson show up and be handed a role. The craziest thing was the producers didn't even make me audition. I guess they figured since I stand upright and speak words on television, I'd do. As excited as I was to have this opportunity, I honestly did not want to disrespect any of the cast members. What they do is extraordinary, and they deserve our admiration and respect.

Enter Deric Rosenblatt, who thankfully agreed to see if he could transform a weather forecaster into someone who wouldn't become the laughingstock of the Great White Way. His spacious but cozy light-filled apartment put me at ease. There was a blanket tossed casually (but oh so artfully) on the sofa. I noticed there was also a rocking chair. I suppose that could be a comfort should one be overcome with emotion while belting out something like "And I'm Telling You I'm Not Going"? When my eyes landed on the baby grand sitting in front of a large window, sunlight streaming over the top of the piano, any comfort I had was gone. I started to feel queasy. Did I need to sit in the rocker?

Deric is a phenomenal voice coach who has worked with recording artists, Grammy, Tony, and Emmy winners—that's just one away from an EGOT, people! One of his clients actually won *The Voice*. Name a Broadway show and most likely one of his students is in it. So what in the hell am I doing here? Just when I was thinking about fleeing the scene, Deric walked in.

"Hi, Al. How are you today? What have you been up to?" Deric sat down at the piano as I started to tell him how thrilled I was that I completed the big project of cleaning out my basement. It was like I had achieved a life goal.

"That's great. I imagine that must be a satisfying feeling!" Deric was playing some notes on the piano. "How long did that project take you?"

I thought for a second. "Honestly, it took forever because my wife doesn't want to throw anything—" *La-la-la-la-la-la*. Was Deric singing? He was!

"Yes, purging can be very hard. And now together." Before I knew what I was doing *la-la-la-la-la-la-la-la* came right out of my mouth. Did Deric and I just sing that together? Before I could think about it any further we had moved on to *mi-mi-mi-mi-mi-mi*.

Whoa. This man tricked me into singing—he's good.

After bewitching me to get me to sing scales, Deric explained that the scales open you up, help relax your voice, and get the most out of the instrument *that is you.*

My job has taken me to the White House, movie sets, science labs, and professional kitchens, but this was the one time my expectations were actually met. Singing in Deric Rosenblatt's studio might be the only time in my life that I thought, Wow, this is just like it is on television.

A few weeks later, after Deric deemed my singing a.k.a. talking on key to be at a level where I wouldn't shame myself, I started working with the head stage manager, Thom Gates, on blocking, lines, and movement.

"Okay. So most of the time you're just sitting at the table in the restaurant at the front of the stage." I was delighted upon reading the script to find that the bulk of my duties would include reading a newspaper and barking out elaborate *When Harry Met Sally*-style orders to the waitress:

"I want pie, and bring me a slice of tomato—but on a separate plate! And orange juice—but not before water, after water! And why are you asking me about potatoes? Did I say anything about potatoes?"

Most of the time I didn't even have to walk to the table; it was perched on a set piece that flew right onto the stage, and then they reeled me back in when the scene was over. But there were a few instances where I did indeed get up.

Thom looked at me with grave concern. "After that scene you get up and move over here. You stand right here."

He was pointing to what appeared to be a completely random spot on the large stage.

"Yes, got it. Right there."

Friday dress rehearsal arrived, and it was just a few scant hours before my Broadway debut. After delivering my line about someone's horoscope (my character loved horoscopes), I stood up to walk over to the random spot on the stage where I was supposed to plant myself. Is it here? No wait, maybe to the left a bit? Just as I was thinking, Oh hell, what do a few inches really matter anyway, my dressing-room mate, Benny Elledge, pulled me upstage just seconds before a wall of scenery came dropping down, landing hard in the exact spot I had been standing.

That was a close one. I guess no one was messing around when they said I must stand "right there."

From that moment on I was memorizing random spots on the stage. I must stand right by that long scratch to avoid being run down by the four-piece band they pull out on a platform, and I should stand right on top of the big gouge so I don't get hit by the diner kitchen that's on wheels. While I knew being on Broadway could result in my utter humiliation, I never anticipated it would be so dangerous. I could just imagine the fun the *Daily News* would have with that headline: "Last Laugh: Al Roker crushed by large set piece traumatizing a thousand people. Coroner says, 'He looks so much flatter in person.'"

Opening night finally rolled around and I was a bundle of nerves. Sure, things could go wrong on live television, but I knew how to ad-lib! I wasn't expected to sing on live television. I was in my dressing room, in costume, prepping myself for the show.

My family was in the audience, as well as my *Today Show* family who had committed to staying up past their bedtimes to support my Broadway debut. I heard the stage manager give the announcement that we were to take our places. I walked over to where I was supposed to be when the curtain opened. My heart started beating like crazy. I realized I had no idea what my first line was. I had no idea what I was supposed to say, on stage, in front of a thousand people in just a few moments.

I didn't know what to do. I wanted to run back to my dressing room and take a look at my script, but there was no time. It's like I was dropped into a nightmare. Why did I do this? Everyone is going to laugh AT me. And just as the panic started to increase to an off-the-charts hurricane level, it came back to me. I remembered exactly what I was supposed to do and what my line was.

That panic was one of the worst feelings I have ever felt. But the bottom line was I had put the work in and deep down—I knew what I was supposed to do. If you put the work in, and then just take a second, chances are whatever you need to know is going to come back to you.

The show went great. I didn't have to shuffle into work cloaked in failure with my colleagues shaking their heads when I walked by. *Broadway, what was he thinking?*

I loved the energy that took place during the show. I can barely describe the feeling of standing on the stage at curtain call, soaking up the applause. I cannot begin to describe the mixture of exhilaration, exhaustion, and gratitude that flooded through me. Being part of such a terrifically talented cast was an honor.

By the way, I've got to say one thing. If you're going to a Broadway show, let's not look like we're going backpacking. You don't have to wear a smoking jacket and a cravat necessarily. But take note, people are dancing and singing for the sake of their lives! Put a smidgeon of effort into it please!

I WAS SURROUNDED by kindness every night. No one begrudged my being a weather personality! My dressing room even had a sofa in it, should the weather guy who gets up at 3:45 A.M. for his day job need to catch a nap (and also, because the role is generally played by folks who are that age where a nap may be required). I loved the experience so much that I harbored fantasies they'd ask me to stay on. *Al, all of the producers agree, you perfectly embody the character of Old Joe. Would you consider staying on indefinitely?* Alas, Old Joe was replaced by Old Josie, and would be played by Broadway veteran June Squibb. My first Broadway run was officially over.

I was so glad that despite my reservations I had said yes. It's important to keep things fresh, whether you're in your first year on the job or your fiftieth. You need to feel that buzz of excitement every day! If you want to continue to excel in your chosen field, make it a point to never stop learning new things. Be open to new interests and follow passions—even if there's no obvious direct correlation between what you'd like to try and how you earn your paycheck. Don't let each day unfold, one after the other, without making an effort to inject new life into whatever it is you do. The second you stop learning is the second you stop getting better.

Fast-forward to a year later, and I was back in my dressing room (hallelujah, hallelujah, the costume still fit) getting ready to play Old Joe again. When I got the call that they wanted me to come back, it's possible I was so excited I busted into a jig. I went back to Deric Rosenblatt, made sure I knew my lines and where to stand so that I wasn't crushed by the moving diner or the band. Five minutes before curtain, I felt really nervous. Those life-sized butterflies were back, but this time I knew it would be okay. Those nerves of mine were there for a reason; they were sending me an important message. Never say no. You never know where it will lead. Take it from an old man!

ALTRUISM #16

Build Your Own
A-Team

HURRICANE DEAN WAS headed to Mexico and Jackie Olensky (an executive producer at *Today*) and Erin Reynolds (a production manager) were flying down to meet me in Cancún. It was the first time we were covering a hurricane in a foreign territory. The usual Cancún vibe of sun, relaxation, and margaritas with tiny umbrellas was nonexistent. The city was quiet, as everyone was bracing for the storm. We drove to Chetumal, which was about five hours away; it's where we expected the hurricane would hit. The area had been evacuated, so we had to pass through a few police checkpoints, which was difficult because sadly, none of us speak Spanish. We managed to get another producer, Danny Noa, on the phone to help translate. "Guys, the authorities want me to make sure you understand that you are entering at your own risk. No one is going to help you." With this warning we forged on and eventually managed to meet up with some other NBC people, and checked into the local Holiday Inn. We got settled and went to sleep. We were all exhausted from the journey.

I woke up in the middle of the night. The wind was really loud, and rain was increasing in intensity to the point that I couldn't see anything out of the window. I knew the eye of the storm was going to pass soon. I got out of bed, quickly got dressed, and threw on my rain gear. I walked down the hallway and knocked on Jackie and Erin's door.

Jackie and I have worked together for many years, and we've really built a connection. She has an innate understanding of what kinds of stories I like, and we're so close at this point that she can write an entire story in my voice. It's kind of spooky. Sometimes it feels like we share the same brain. This explains why when Jackie opened the door and saw my face, we basically had an entire conversation telepathically—no speaking whatsoever.

> JACKIE: Oh, hell no, Roker. I know you did not just wake me up in the middle of the night after a five-hour drive to see if I want to endanger my life by going outside moments before a hurricane hits. Do you have any idea how tired I am? Do you understand that I wish to live to see tomorrow?

> > ME: Well, yeah—but we flew all the way here, and then there was that long drive! And hello! We had to cross police checkpoints! And for what? To sit safely in this hotel while all the action is taking place right outside?

> JACKIE: How is it even possible you've been forecasting the weather for years and you are

even contemplating this? Do you not remember being blown down on national television by Hurricane Wilma in front of the entire country? Are you even aware that BuzzFeed did an article called "Seven Weathermen Blown Away by Hurricanes" and you make up most of the list? When will you ever learn? When you're blown halfway out into the ocean? Don't expect me to come fish you out, by the way.

Jackie kept staring at me, stony faced. She shook her head slightly back and forth as if to say, *Don't say it, Al. Do. Not. Even. Say. It. You're going to say it, aren't you?*

She was right, I ended our silent conversation when I blurted out: "Good morning! Well, almost! So, hey, guys, what's up? You want to go outside and check out the storm? Sounds like things are really kicking up out there!"

Jackie continued shaking her head like she couldn't have been more disappointed if I had hotwired her car and hot-rodded around town with it until I crashed it, only to find out the trunk was full of her grandmother's china. She finally spoke:

"Uh no, Al!"

She calmly closed the door. Okay! Message received. I was left alone in the hallway to ponder my behavior like a disruptive school kid. Was it wrong to suggest hurricane watching at 3:00 A.M.?

I started walking back to my room when I heard what sounded like an explosion—*Whoa, what was that?* I turned around and saw Jackie and Erin come out of their room. Oh, have they changed their minds? Great!

Jackie looked concerned and she jumped right into action. "Al, the windows are blown in. We need to take cover. Now." We quickly determined the hallway was the safest spot. We spent the next three hours hunkered down together trying to keep safe from shattering windows.

Jackie is one of my biggest supporters, and I don't know how I'd manage without her (i.e., *be alive* without her). But if I have a crazy idea, she'll be the first person to let me know. Had she said, "Yeah, sure, by all means! Let's go outside at 3:00 A.M. to 'check out' the massive hurricane that could potentially kill us all. What a terrific idea!" it's possible that things could have ended badly. Jackie doesn't suffer fools and she doesn't hesitate to tell me if I'm about to make a big mistake. Jackie is a fantastic producer, but ultimately she just has much more sense than I do. While we were sitting in a hallway together for hours trying to avoid flying glass, I couldn't help but think, Roker, remember this moment, and for God's sake from now on listen to Jackie and ignore most of your own instincts! I can't stress this enough—to achieve massive, long-term success at work, *align yourself with someone who has more sense than you do.*

Jackie has been an absolutely crucial part of my crew, my posse, my squad . . . *my A-Team.*

EACH AND EVERY MORNING, as I'm walking into my dressing room I say the same thing aloud: "Alexa, play theme from *The A-Team.*" As the snare drum beats out its sound, I recite the lines from the opening monologue:

> In 1972, a crack commando unit was sent to prison by a military court for a crime they didn't commit. These men promptly escaped from a maximum-security stockade to the Los Angeles underground. Today, still wanted by the government, they survive as soldiers of fortune. If you have a problem, if no one else can help, and if you can find them, maybe you can hire . . . the A-Team.

My version of the A-Team (or should I say R-Team) isn't technically a "crack commando unit." To the best of my knowledge no one has escaped from prison* or lived underground, and the only war we have waged has been

---

*Although Carson Daly has a lot of tattoos. He's covered in them underneath that well-cut suit.

the battle of the Morning Television Shows. I credit my A-Team for my success. My A-Team inspires me, keeps my spirits up, keeps me on my toes, keeps me sane, and makes it a lot easier to show up for work at the crack of dawn. The right team can provide you with the peace of mind that together you can tackle anything: long hours, difficult co-workers, an attempted kidnapping, or maybe an alien takeover (be ready for anything). You never know, people! The bottom line is that if you create your own A-Team you'll always have the right support. Your personal A-Team may need to be tailored to whatever job you do to bring home the bacon, but after decades of work experience I suggest that you cast the following roles.

A human BS detector and a stealth interrogator:

I walk into the dressing room and I plop down in the chair next to Hoda, and for the next twenty minutes I get caught up in the wonderful mix that is the news of the day with a side dish of caustic commentary, as well as the latest doings of Savannah's brood, plus the childhood milestones of Haley Joy and Hope. While I'm listening to the most important ladies in my professional life talk about motherhood and work, I'll nod and smile, occasionally saying something to let them know what a great job they're doing with their kids. What they don't know is that while they're being powdered and hair sprayed I'm thinking, My God—if we ever needed to foil an evil billionaire's plot to buy up a small American town that's unknowingly perched on top of a massive untapped oil field, these ladies could handle it. No problem.

Hoda's smile is bright enough to power a jet (or any other flying vehicle that could be used for escape, which could come in handy), but she also has the best bullshit detector I've ever encountered. If Hoda detects the presence of even the tiniest red flag, there's no doubt about it—there's something treacherous afoot. Hoda is like the canary in the coal mine when it comes to bad-tricky-potentially-complicated situations. There is no getting anything past Hoda. Give her a glass of "nice" wine and she'll immediately call me out on it after just one sip. "Roker? Why are you serving me this fancy-pants wine? Don't you know that the $15 rosé tastes just as good?" And it's for reasons like this that I value her take on everything from book recommendations to how to stop criminal masterminds (and obviously bargain wines). Having someone at work whose thoughts you trust implicitly is a true gift. I recommend you find such a person and ply them with treats to keep yourself in their favor. "Siri. Make a note to send Hoda flowers, chocolate, and a case of wine."

When Savannah arrived on *The Today Show* set armed with her impeccable journalistic credentials and juris doctorate from one of the nation's finest law schools, I couldn't help but wonder what she would think of the rest of us nutjobs. This is *The Today Show* where cooking on live television is de rigueur! And surely an attorney would know that "wine o'clock" isn't a real time. Savannah is funny, polite, and incredibly poised, but oh, do not mistake all that positive energy for someone who just wants to engage in light chitchat over tea and scones because you'll go down, my friend. You'll go down hard. Savannah can certainly conduct an interview with sensitivity and compassion, as she often does, but know that when the situation calls for it, she's the most thorough and fierce interviewer I have ever encountered. It's like when her law background was mixed with her journalistic experience it formed an impenetrable shield around her. No one can stop Savannah once she gets going. She'll keep moving ahead until she gets the necessary information. If her favorite post-show snack disappeared from the break room (guacamole), God help us all. Savannah would be interrogating each and every one of us. *When were you last in the break room? Are you currently or have you ever been in possession of tortilla chips, carrot sticks, or celery that were screaming to be dipped in something?* The questioning would continue until the guacamole thief was found. An evil billionaire would stand no chance against Savannah; she'd get to the truth behind his plot in about six seconds, and the best part would be he'd never see it coming. Someone in your work circle who digs deep and gets to the bottom of any situation is an incredible ally to have—be sure to stay on their good side.

A really, really good-looking guy:

While I'm waiting for the makeup team to do their magic (thanks to my advanced age and bald head, it takes a total of thirty seconds and *I'm ready for my close-up, Mr. DeMille!*), Craig waltzes in—looking annoyingly perfect. He'll grab a yogurt, sit down, and start sending tweets. I can't help but stare; how does he always look so fresh faced and youthful? And at this hour? "Al, why are you looking at me like that?" My God, this man is positively glowing. There's no doubt about it, if I ever needed to penetrate an elite organization in order to save the country from peril (or get a table in a trendy restaurant where I forgot to make a reservation), it's Craig and his magnetic face I'd want by my side.

An example of schadenfreude:

A job that has no bad days does not exist, and the sooner you understand this the better (a job is not a party, not even for the business owners). If this unicorn of a job actually existed, there would be no such thing as weekends or songs like "Nine to Five" by Dolly Parton or "Take This Job and Shove It" by Johnny Paycheck (ironic last name there). It's not my general policy to use the misfortune of others to make myself feel better, but I can't help but think about Joe Mosbrook when I'm having a really bad day.

I worked with Joe Mosbrook back in Cleveland. One afternoon Joe was out in the field covering a breaking story. After they wrapped up, he got in the helicopter to go back to the station. The helicopter crashed immediately after takeoff. This could have been a real tragedy, but amazingly, no one was hurt. Joe popped out of the smoldering wreckage, disheveled and shocked, but okay, literally brushed himself off and then proceeded to do *a breaking news story about his own helicopter crash. The very one he had just walked away from.* We all have those days that just make you wish life had a reset button. But chances are your day is a field of peonies compared to someone else's. And if you aren't covering your own accident on the news, was it really *that bad?* I'm not suggesting you start littering the street with banana peels so you can laugh at people when they slip, but have a memory you can pull out of your pocket that lightens your mood and keeps you calm. Refer to that memory when you're facing a mini-drama, brush off whatever's bothering you, and move on with it all.

Your own Professor X:

A remarkable thing about Willard Scott was that as I moved up the ladder he never viewed me as competition (everyone frets about the competition in this biz). Like Professor X and his team of mutants, Willard viewed my talent and potential as a gift—something to be cultivated and encouraged, not beaten down and squashed from existence. Willard used his powers for good! Willard generously extended a hand, provided advice, urged me to keep on going—and was always a friend. If someone with more experience than you offers mentorship, inspiration, or advice—take it with gratitude. It's not every day that you meet an ultra-powerful mutant king who can help you cultivate your skills!

Sitting there in the dressing room while Savannah and Hoda get gussied up and Craig finally finishes his yogurt I feel like all is right in my work universe, because I have one hell of an A-Team. With over forty years of work experience under my now smaller belt, I've learned a few things. Whether you're delivering the news or you're involved in a top-secret mission that entails riding around in a kick-ass van, dodging explosions, and firing off more rounds of ammunition than are shot off in most small South American wars, when it comes to building a career you've got to rely on other people. You can't fly solo. As

Hannibal Smith says at the end of "Deadly Maneuvers" in season two of *The A-Team*, standing over his defeated adversary: "Next time you wanna take someone out, don't get yourself a good squad. Get yourself a team!" You need a team to successfully execute any mission, and that mission is going to be full of unexpected detours, breakdowns, and surprises no matter how well you plan ahead. And here's one of life's biggest secrets—most plans only come together in retrospect.

AFTER THE A-TEAM completed another successful explosion-filled operation, Hannibal, the mastermind of the group, would light up a cigar and say, "I love it when a plan comes together." Who doesn't? I urge you to have dreams and ideas. Big ones! Imagine the places you want to go to and the things you want to learn and accomplish, but allow your life to unfold. Don't concern yourself with creating a perfect foolproof plan, because there is simply no such thing. The unexpected is inevitable. Everything won't go the way you want it to and it will become a little absurd at times, but that doesn't mean you won't end up exactly where you want to be. Be open to moving to a far-flung locale (like Cleveland!), try out that less than perfect job—and go ahead and buy that lime-green suit with the reversible vest. And wear it! The disappointments will come, but so will the surprises—the mentor who lifts you up, the boss who pushes you to be better, the colleague who helps you shine and be your best self. There will be times when you don't think you'll ever get from point A to point B. It's too hard, the path is too uncertain—people are constantly swearing at you! But the sky always clears eventually, and you'll find you are right where you wanted to be. You will look back on every moment with gladness and appreciation, and you'll think, *I love it when a plan comes together.*

A Storm Doesn't Have to Sink Your Ship

I'VE SPENT ALMOST fifty years covering hurricanes, floods, snowstorms, and tornadoes—some of the most dangerous weather situations Mother Nature has thrown our way. If I've learned anything over these past few decades, it's that even with the best technology and the most up-to-date data, sometimes you can't always predict how big a storm is going to be or how long it will last. And even when we had the first inklings that a pandemic might be on the horizon in January and February 2020, I don't think anyone could've predicted how incredibly difficult the year would turn out to be—on so many levels. As of this writing, more than half a million Americans have lost their lives to COVID-19, families are grieving, and many others have lost their businesses and livelihoods. The darkness brought on by this pandemic has been unfathomable and all-encompassing.

In fact, I was so focused on the pandemic that when my physician, Dr. Michael Farber, expressed concern over an elevated PSA level (an indicator of prostate cancer) during my routine checkup that same year, I wasn't particularly concerned. It seemed inconsequential when all of our lives had changed so drastically. After a subsequent MRI ordered by my new urologist, Dr. Michael Stifelman, didn't show anything abnormal, my doctor scheduled a biopsy. The day I had an appointment to get the results,

I remained unworried. I'd spent the last few months in quarantine with my family, feeling blessed that we were able to be together but anxious to keep us safe from the virus that was sickening Americans by the millions. Cancer just wasn't on my mind.

When I arrived at Stifelman's office, he shut the door and said, "I prefer to give this kind of news in person." My mindset shifted immediately: well, that doesn't sound good. He went on to say, "We got the results. You have prostate cancer." My first thought? *Deborah is going to kill me.* I knew she would have wanted to be there to provide support. Deborah had originally offered to accompany me to the appointment, but I'd already managed to convince myself that *everything was fine! Nothing to worry about here!* I felt there was no need for her to come along. I would have made a different decision had I known that while I was leaving my house healthy that morning, I'd be coming home as a cancer patient.

After a series of second opinions, discussions about radiation and chemotherapy, and lots of soul-searching, I opted for surgery. Dr. Vincent Laudone at Memorial Sloan Kettering, a leading expert in the field, said the surgery went well, and my family and I were relieved to learn five months later that my PSA level was down to 0.05, meaning that prostate cancer was no longer detectable.

Still, I'll continue to get blood work done every six months for the next five years to make sure I'm in the clear. I *know* how fortunate I am. Black men have a 50 percent higher chance of developing prostate cancer and are twice as likely to die from the disease. Because I had access to screening and health care, my cancer was identified early. For me, the most uncomfortable part of this entire process was standing in line at the pharmacy with a big pack of man diapers! I admit I felt self-conscious. *Is everyone looking at me holding these adult diapers?* No one cared. I could have been buying a year's supply of gum, and no one would have noticed. I am pleased to report that everything is now in working order! Bottom line for all my fellow gentlemen out there (no pun intended): get to the doctor, get screened, and get your baseline PSA tested so you can protect yourself and live your best life. After all, it's a lot easier to stay dry if you grab an umbrella when it just starts sprinkling outside; it's significantly harder to make it through a full-on thunderstorm without getting drenched.

LUCKILY FOR ME, the past year or so hasn't been all bad, and I was proud to be able to attend the inauguration of President Joe Biden in January 2021. Thanks to my work on *The Today Show,* I've had the privilege of meeting several presidents, and it's always a thrill. When Leila was a toddler, during the Clinton years, we were in the Oval Office;

later on, in 2006, we were on the lawn of the White House with President and Mrs. Bush. In 2008, when Barack and Michelle Obama marched down Pennsylvania Avenue in the inaugural parade, the streets were packed with cheering onlookers. President Obama, at the urging of Mrs. Obama, told me how good he was feeling as he marched toward the White House. And when our new then vice president Joe Biden approached, I shouted out to him and was rewarded with a high-energy handshake from Mr. Vice President himself! The energy and excitement on the street during that inauguration was extraordinary, and I had never felt anything like it.

Inauguration Day 2021, however, was notably different. The streets were kept free of onlookers, the parade was mostly virtual, and extreme precautions were taken to keep everyone safe because of the pandemic. As I was standing by the side of the street, quieter than any inaugural parade I've been to, I perked up as I saw Joe Biden, now our forty-sixth president, walking down the street with his wife, Dr. Jill Biden. This time, I shouted out, "Mr. President! Mr. President!" President Biden started walking toward me, and I'm thinking, *Is this really happening?* Our newly elected president came over to give me a fist bump and said, "We've got to keep doing this." I smiled (okay, fine, I jumped up and down like a five-year-old on Christmas) as I watched our new president moving forward down the parade route, ready to take on one of the hardest jobs in the world during an incredibly difficult period in our history.

As President Biden walked off, I kept thinking about the power, as well as the many shades of meaning, behind his words: "We've got to keep doing this." Sure, I'd love another chance to high-five or fist-bump the president (who wouldn't?!), but it goes deeper than that. No matter what kind of storm life throws at us—a hurricane, a cancer diagnosis, a pandemic, a job loss—we've got to keep doing *what we do.* A storm doesn't have to sink your ship! It is hard to keep your balance when big waves crash into you, but if you get back up, you may find that you can stand up—and, what's more, you can *keep* standing, holding your ground in that middle place, even if you can't move forward. Of course, I'm not suggesting you ignore the pain and hardship during this unprecedented time, but if you are strong enough to stay in that middle place, you can let everything wash over you…the good and the bad. When it comes down to it, what's the alternative? Do you really want to get tossed overboard into the murky water with the sharks and schools of poisonous jellyfish? *I'll pass on that, thanks.*

And hey, sometimes, there are bright spots to be seen from the middle place! Some are like a small sliver of light; for example, the ultra-nerdy AV skills I honed in high school allowed me to build a makeshift studio during the pandemic so I could still broadcast the weather for

The Today Show from the safety of my own home. I also wasn't traveling for work anymore, which was a huge change. This opened up time to slow down and connect with my family. My son, Nick, and I created our very own YouTube show called *What We're Cooking!*, where we roasted chicken, grilled burgers, and tried our hands at Asian-style short ribs. I grew my own cherry tomatoes and herbs, and I started composting our scraps. My family rediscovered the joy of the pop-o-matic (such a satisfying sound!) while playing Trouble. I really cherished this unforeseen extra time to spend with the people I love most.

It also reminded me not to take things for granted and to really appreciate those special moments, the ones that are on par with a bright, sunny day. Due to travel restrictions, I didn't see my daughter Leila for almost a year, so when she was able to visit for Christmas, it was the best gift I could have asked for. My older daughter, Courtney, got engaged in 2020, and as a family we've been able to share the joy (and all the complications) of planning a wedding during a pandemic. My appreciation for Deborah, too, has reached entirely new heights. Whenever I was down, Deborah stayed positive and was there for me. When Deborah was feeling low, I was able to help lift her up. I am incredibly grateful that we were never down at the same time; through and through, she is my lifeline. I'm extra fortunate in that regard; I know that some of you have had to weather this storm on your own, which can be a serious challenge, and I mean it when I say my thoughts are with you.

The year 2020 will always be the year the pandemic hit—and the year I became a cancer patient. I think we were all grateful to ring in 2021, but even though a new year has started and hope is on the horizon, we're still adjusting to our new reality—social distancing and mask wearing are our new normal, while we hold out hope that the COVID-19 vaccines will one day restore our lives to some degree of what they looked like before. Throughout all of this, I've never doubted that I am blessed, but a cancer diagnosis and a pandemic have shown me just how important it is to find that middle place when things get tough—and stick to it. There is power in just *doing what we do*. When it all starts to feel like too much, we must remember to just do what we do and keep *living*: take walks, "go to work," call friends, prepare meals, cry!, check on neighbors, and face each day as it comes. We can just take it one day at a time, and once that storm has passed, we'll be stronger. I may not know what the rest of the year looks like, or even the years ahead of us, but this much I know: no matter what happens, no matter how difficult life gets, always look for that middle place so you can wait out the storm. It's from this very middle place that we'll be able to enjoy all the blessings the future has in store for us.

Acknowledgments

There are many people who, in one way or another, had a profound impact on my life and therefore helped shape this book.

Dr. Louis B. O'Donnell who saw something in me that I didn't see in myself back in 1972 at SUNY Oswego. I will be forever grateful.

Meeting and being befriended by Willard Scott has been one of the greatest joys and privileges of my life. He is truly the gift that keeps giving.

My beloved parents, Al and Isabel Roker, instilled in me a love of life and a work ethic that drives me to this day, and I will forever love and miss them. I fall short of who they were but try and be that parent, spouse, and friend each day.

My siblings, Alisa, Desireé, Patricia, and Chris are my cheerleaders and a point of pride that gives me sustenance. They are the greatest posse a brother could ever ask for. I lucked into my life. They earned theirs.

My children; Courtney, Leila, and Nicholas are the reason I try to be a better person and father and as a bonus, be as embarrassing a Dad as possible. A father could not be prouder or more blessed than having these three children call me father.

And to Deborah Roberts, each day I thank God for your wisdom, forbearance, humor, guidance, and love. Even though I know I drive you crazy, I hope you enjoy the ride.

A lot of folks helped make this book a reality. I want to thank the fine folks at Hachette, Michael Barrs, Sarah Falter, Mary Ann Naples, Carrie Napolitano, and Mollie Weisenfeld. I especially want to thank Krishan Trotman who first approached me with the idea for this tome.

A big thank you to Mel Berger, my literary agent at WME. I still can't believe I have a literary agent. Of course, I wouldn't without my overall guiding light at WME, Jon Rosen.

Helping me organize this whole mishigas was Paula Balzer Vitale who with grace, humor, and patience, provided a lot of insight and more importantly, laughs. And thanks to my assistants, Anndi Liggett and Taylor Knight, who prodded, cajoled, and kept me on schedule.

And to all the terrific writers, producers, photojournalists, executives, and on-air talent who made me who and what I am today, America can blame you.

As I advance in age, memory starts to fade so if I forgot to mention you, buy a fine point Sharpie (I will reimburse you) and you can write your name in the space provided.

I couldn't have written this book or had the career I've enjoyed without the invaluable assistance of _____
_____.

Made in the USA
Monee, IL
12 June 2023